Fix-It and Forget-It®

KETO COMFORT FOOD

Cookbook

127 SUPER EASY SLOW COOKER MEALS

HOPE COMERFORD

Good Books

New York, New York

Table of Contents

Welcome to Fix-It and Forget-It Keto Comfort Food Cookbook

If you're following a keto diet, then this book is going to be a life-saver! It's filled with many of your favorite comfort foods, which all fit within keto guidelines. We're bringing you things like savory soups like Broccoli-Cheese Soup, delicious dinners like Chicken Cacciatore and Lasagna, delicious breakfast frittatas and omelets, and even amazing desserts like Raspberry Custard and Chocolate Almond Cake!

Being on a diet doesn't mean you have to do without the foods you love! Our hope is that this book takes the guessing out of what to make each day and helps keep you within your dietary guidelines.

What Is the Keto Diet?

The keto diet involves eating foods high in fat and low in carbs. By lowering the level of carbs you are eating and increasing the amount of fat you're eating to replace the carbs, your body starts goes into a metabolic state known as ketosis. You will also find this is a no-sugar diet. There are several natural (plant-based) sweeteners recommended for those following a keto diet, and you will see those throughout the book in various recipes.

It is also said that by following a keto diet, your blood sugar and insulin levels decrease dramatically. Many have received major health benefits by following this diet, including weight loss.

As always, it is recommended that you consult your physician before beginning any diet to make sure it is the right choice for you. If you choose to follow this diet, we hope you have great success and that this book helps you along your journey.

Nutrition information included with each recipe is approximate. Any ingredients listed as "optional" or under "serving suggestions" or "variations" are not included in the nutrition analysis.

Choosing a Slow Cooker

Not all slow cookers are created equal . . . or work equally as well for everyone!

Those of us who use slow cookers frequently know we have our own preferences when it comes to which slow cooker we choose to use. For instance, I love my programmable slow cooker, but there are many programmable slow cookers I've tried that I've strongly disliked. Why? Because some go by increments of 15 or 30 minutes and some go by 4, 6, 8, or 10 hours. I dislike those restrictions, but I have family and friends who don't mind them at all! I am also pretty brand loyal when it comes to my manual slow cookers because I've had great success with those and have had unsuccessful moments with slow cookers of other brands. So, which slow cooker(s) is/are best for your household?

It really depends on how many people you're feeding and if you're gone for long periods of time. Here are my recommendations:

For 2–3 person household	3–5 quart slow cooker
For 4–5 person household	5–6 quart slow cooker
For a 6+ person household	6½–7 quart slow cooker

Large slow cooker advantages/disadvantages:

Advantages:
- You can fit a loaf pan or a baking dish into a 6- or 7-quart, depending on the shape of your cooker. That allows you to make bread or cakes, or even smaller quantities of main dishes. (Take your favorite baking dish and loaf pan along when you shop for a cooker to make sure they'll fit inside.)
- You can feed large groups of people, or make larger quantities of food, allowing for leftovers, or meals, to freeze.

Disadvantages:
- They take up more storage room.
- They don't fit as neatly into a dishwasher.
- If your crock isn't ⅔–¾ full, you may burn your food.

Small slow cooker advantages/disadvantages:

Advantages:
- They're great for lots of appetizers, for serving hot drinks, for baking cakes straight in the crock, and for dorm rooms or apartments.
- Great option for making recipes of smaller quantities.

Disadvantages:
- Food in smaller quantities tends to cook more quickly than larger amounts. So keep an eye on it.
- Chances are, you won't have many leftovers. So, if you like to have leftovers, a smaller slow cooker may not be a good option for you.

My recommendation:

Have at least two slow cookers; one around 3 to 4 quarts and one 6 quarts or larger. A third would be a huge bonus (and a great advantage to your cooking repertoire!). The advantage of having at least a couple is you can make a larger variety of recipes. Also, you can make at least two or three dishes at once for a whole meal.

Manual vs. Programmable

If you are gone for only six to eight hours a day, a manual slow cooker might be just fine for you. If you are gone for more than eight hours during the day, I would highly recommend purchasing a programmable slow cooker that will switch to warm when the cook time you set is up. It will allow you to cook a wider variety of recipes.

The two I use most frequently are my 4-quart manual slow cooker and my 6½-quart programmable slow cooker. I like that I can make smaller portions in my 4-quart slow cooker on days I don't need or want leftovers, but I also love how my 6½-quart slow cooker can accommodate whole chickens, turkey breasts, hams, or big batches of soups. I use them both often.

Get to know your slow cooker . . .

Plan a little time to get acquainted with your slow cooker. Each slow cooker has its own personality—just like your oven (and your car). Plus, many new slow cookers cook hotter and faster than earlier models. I think that with all of the concern for food safety, the slow cooker manufacturers have amped up their settings so that "High," "Low," and "Warm" are all higher temperatures than in the older models. That means they cook hotter—and therefore, faster—than the first slow cookers. The beauty of these little machines is that they're supposed to cook low and slow. We count on that when we flip the switch in the morning before we leave the house for ten hours or so. So, because none of us knows what kind of temperament our slow cooker has until we try it out, nor how hot it cooks—don't assume anything. Save yourself a disappointment and make the first recipe in your new slow cooker on a day when you're at home. Cook it for the shortest amount of time the recipe calls for. Then, check the food to see if it's done. Or if you start smelling food that seems to be finished, turn off the cooker and rescue your food.

Also, all slow cookers seem to have a "hot spot," which is of great importance to know, especially when baking with your slow cooker. This spot may tend to burn food in that area if you're not careful. If you're baking directly in your slow cooker, I recommend covering the "hot spot" with some foil.

Take notes . . .

Don't be afraid to make notes in your cookbook. It's yours! Chances are, it will eventually get passed down to someone in your family and they will love and appreciate all of your musings. Take note of which slow cooker you used and exactly how long it took to cook the recipe. The next time you make it, you won't need to try to remember. Apply what you learned to the next recipes you make in your cooker. If another recipe says it needs to cook 7–9 hours, and you've discovered your slow cooker cooks on the faster side, cook that recipe for 6–6½ hours and then check it. You can always cook a recipe longer—but you can't reverse things if it's overdone.

Get creative . . .

If you know your morning is going to be hectic, prepare everything the night before, take it out so the crock warms up to room temperature when you first get up in the morning, then plug it in and turn it on as you're leaving the house.

If you want to make something that has a short cook time and you're going to be gone longer than that, cook it the night before and refrigerate it for the next day. Warm it up when you get home. Or, cook those recipes on the weekend when you know you'll be home and eat them later in the week.

Slow Cooking Tips and Tricks and Other Things You May Not Know

- Slow cookers tend to work best when they're ½ to ¾ of the way full. You may need to increase the cooking time if you've exceeded that amount, or reduce it if you've put in less than that. If you're going to exceed that limit, it would be best to reduce the recipe, or split it between two slow cookers. (Remember how I suggested owning at least two or three slow cookers?)

- Keep your veggies on the bottom. That puts them in more direct contact with the heat. The fuller your slow cooker, the longer it will take its contents to cook. Also, the more densely packed the cooker's contents are, the longer they will take to cook. And finally, the larger the chunks of meat or vegetables, the more time they will need to cook.

- Keep the lid on! Every time you take a peek, you lose 20 minutes of cooking time. Please take this into consideration each time you lift the lid! I know, some of you can't help yourself and are going to lift anyway. Just don't forget to tack on 20 minutes to your cook time for each time you peeked!

- Sometimes it's beneficial to remove the lid. If you'd like your dish to thicken a bit, take the lid off during the last half hour to hour of cooking time.

- If you have a big slow cooker (7- to 8-quart), you can cook a small batch in it by putting the recipe ingredients into an oven-safe baking dish or baking pan and then placing that into the cooker's crock. First, put a trivet or some metal jar rings on the bottom of the crock, and then set your dish or pan on top of them. Or a loaf pan may "hook onto" the top ridges of the crock belonging to a large oval cooker and hang there straight and securely, "baking" a cake or quick bread. Cover the cooker and flip it on.

- The outside of your slow cooker will be hot! Please remember to keep it out of reach of children and keep that in mind for yourself as well!

- Get yourself a quick-read meat thermometer and use it! This helps remove the question of whether or not your meat is fully cooked, and helps prevent you from overcooking your meat as well.

  Internal Cooking Temperatures:
  - Beef—125–130°F (rare); 140–145°F (medium); 160°F (well-done)
  - Pork—140–145°F (rare); 145–150°F (medium); 160°F (well-done)
  - Turkey and Chicken—165°F
  - Frozen meat: The basic rule of thumb is, don't put frozen meat into the slow cooker. The meat does not reach the proper internal temperature in time. This especially applies to thick cuts of meat! Proceed with caution!

- Add fresh herbs 10 minutes before the end of the cooking time to maximize their flavor.
- If your recipe calls for cooked pasta, add it 10 minutes before the end of the cooking time if the cooker is on High; 30 minutes before the end of the cooking time if it's on Low. Then the pasta won't get mushy.
- If your recipe calls for sour cream or cream, stir it in 5 minutes before the end of the cooking time. You want it to heat but not boil or simmer.

Approximate Slow Cooker Temperatures (Remember, each slow cooker is different):

- Low—170°F–200°F
- Simmer—185°F
- Warm—165°F

Cooked and dried bean measurements:

- 16-oz. can, drained = about 1¾ cups beans
- 19-oz. can, drained = about 2 cups beans
- 1 lb. dried beans (about 2½ cups) = 5 cups cooked beans

Breakfast

Fresh Veggie and Herb Omelet

Hope Comerford, Clinton Township, MI

Makes 8 servings
Prep. Time: 20 minutes ❧ Cooking Time: 4–6 hours ❧ Ideal slow-cooker size: 6-qt.

12 eggs

1 cup unsweetened almond milk or whole milk

½ tsp. kosher salt

¼ tsp. pepper

3 cloves garlic, minced

1 tsp. fresh chopped basil

6 dashes Frank's RedHot

2 cups broccoli florets

1 yellow bell pepper, diced

1 red bell pepper, diced

1 medium onion, diced

1 cup crumbled feta cheese

1 cup diced cherry tomatoes

½ fresh chopped parsley

1. Spray crock with nonstick spray.

2. In a bowl, mix together the eggs, milk, salt, pepper, garlic, basil, and hot sauce.

3. Place the broccoli, yellow pepper, red pepper, and onion in crock. Gently mix with a spoon.

4. Pour egg mixture over the top.

5. Cover and cook on Low for 4–6 hours, or until center is set.

6. Sprinkle feta over the top, then cook an additional 30 minutes.

7. To serve, sprinkle the omelet with the chopped tomatoes and fresh parsley.

- Calories 197
- Fat 12
- Sodium 456
- Carbs 9
- Sugar 4
- Protein 14

Vegetable Omelet

Phyllis Good, Lancaster, PA

Makes 4–6 servings
Prep. Time: 20 minutes ⚜ Cooking Time: 2 hours ⚜ Ideal slow-cooker size: 6-quart

5 eggs
⅓ cup whole milk
¼ tsp. salt
pinch black pepper
⅓ cup chopped onion
1 clove garlic, minced
1 cup small broccoli florets
1 cup thinly sliced zucchini
½ cup thinly sliced red bell pepper
½ cup your favorite grated cheese

1. Beat eggs with milk, salt, and pepper.

2. Add onion, garlic, broccoli, zucchini, and bell pepper. Stir.

3. Pour mixture into lightly greased baking dish that will fit in your slow cooker. Set dish on a small trivet or jar rings in slow cooker.

4. Cover and cook on High for 2 hours, until eggs are set and vegetables are softened.

5. Sprinkle with cheese and allow to melt before serving. Carefully, wearing oven mitts, remove hot dish from hot slow cooker. Slice and serve.

- Calories 108
- Fat 6
- Sodium 272
- Carbs 5
- Sugar 2
- Protein 8

Crustless Chicken and Spinach Quiche

Phyllis Good, Lancaster, PA

Makes 6 servings
Prep. Time: 20 minutes ⚶ Cooking Time: 1½–2 hours
Standing Time: 20–30 minutes ⚶ Ideal slow-cooker size: 5-quart

I cup chopped, cooked chicken

I cup shredded Swiss cheese

½ cup cooked, chopped spinach, drained (about ⅓ of a 10-oz. frozen pkg., thawed)

¼ cup chopped onion

2 eggs

¾ cup mayonnaise

¾ cup whole milk

⅛ tsp. pepper

1. In a good-sized bowl, mix together chicken, cheese, spinach, and onion.

2. Grease the inside of your crock with nonstick cooking spray. Spread the contents of the bowl around the inside of the crock.

3. In same bowl, stir together eggs, mayonnaise, milk, and pepper until smooth.

4. Pour over chicken-spinach mixture.

5. Cover. Cook on High 1½–2 hours, or until knife inserted into center of quiche comes out clean.

6. Uncover quickly, swooping lid away from yourself so no water drips on quiche from the inside of the lid.

- Calories 305
- Fat 22
- Sodium 736
- Carbs 8
- Sugar 3
- Protein 21

Italian Frittata

Hope Comerford, Clinton Township, MI

Makes 6 servings
Prep. Time: 10 minutes ♣ Cooking Time: 3–4 hours ♣ Ideal slow-cooker size: 5- or 6-qt.

10 eggs
1 Tbsp. chopped fresh basil
1 Tbsp. chopped fresh mint
1 Tbsp. chopped fresh sage
1 Tbsp. chopped fresh oregano
½ tsp. sea salt
⅛ tsp. pepper
1 Tbsp. grated Parmesan cheese
¼ cup diced prosciutto
½ cup chopped onion

1. Spray your crock with nonstick spray.

2. In a bowl, mix together the eggs, basil, mint, sage, oregano, sea salt, pepper, and Parmesan. Pour this mixture into the crock.

3. Sprinkle the prosciutto and onion evenly over the egg mixture in the crock.

4. Cover and cook on Low for 3–4 hours.

Serving suggestion:
Serve with fresh fruit and/or keto toast.

- Calories 137
- Fat 9
- Sodium 327
- Carbs 2
- Sugar 1
- Protein 12

Spinach Fritatta

Shirley Unternahrer, Wayland, IA

Makes 4–6 servings
Prep. Time: 15 minutes ⚜ *Cooking Time: 1½–2 hours* ⚜ *Ideal slow-cooker size: 5-qt.*

4 eggs

½ tsp. kosher salt

½ tsp. dried basil

fresh ground pepper, to taste

3 cups chopped fresh spinach, stems removed

½ cup chopped tomato, liquid drained off

⅓ cup freshly grated Parmesan cheese

1. Whisk eggs well in mixing bowl. Whisk in salt, basil, and pepper.

2. Gently stir in spinach, tomato, and Parmesan.

3. Pour into lightly greased slow cooker.

4. Cover and cook on High for 1½–2 hours, until middle is set. Serve hot.

- Calories 69
- Fat 4
- Sodium 300
- Carbs 2
- Sugar 0.5
- Protein 6

Crustless Spinach Quiche

Barbara Hoover, Landisville, PA
Barbara Jean Fabel, Wausau, WI

Makes 8 servings
Prep. Time: 10 minutes ⚘ *Cooking Time: 4–6 hours* ⚘ *Ideal slow-cooker size: 3-qt.*

2 (10-oz.) pkgs. frozen chopped spinach, squeezed dry

2 cups cottage cheese

¼ cup butter, cut into pieces

1½ cups sharp cheddar cheese, cubed

3 eggs, beaten

¼ cup almond flour

1 tsp. salt

1. Combine ingredients thoroughly.

2. Pour into a greased slow cooker. Cover.

3. Cook on Low 4–6 hours.

NOTE
Recipe may be doubled for a 5-qt. slow cooker.
—Barbara Jean Fabel

- Calories 261
- Fat 21
- Sodium 718
- Carbs 6
- Sugar 3
- Protein 14

Breakfast Bake

Kristi See, Weskan, KS

Makes 10 servings
Prep Time: 15 minutes ❧ *Cooking Time: 3–4 hours* ❧ *Ideal slow-cooker size: 4- to 5-qt.*

12 eggs
1½–2 cups grated cheese, your choice
1 cup diced cooked ham
1 cup whole milk
1 tsp. salt
½ tsp. pepper

1. Beat eggs. Pour into slow cooker.

2. Mix in remaining ingredients.

3. Cover and cook on Low 3–4 hours.

- Calories 223
- Fat 15
- Sodium 654
- Carbs 2.5
- Sugar 1.5
- Protein 18

Shirred Eggs

Margaret W. High, Lancaster, PA

Makes 4 servings
Prep. Time: 20 minutes   ❧   Cooking Time: 2 hours   ❧   Ideal slow-cooker size: 4–5 qt.

4 eggs, room temperature
1 Tbsp. butter
Salt and pepper, to taste

1. Have ready a shallow baking dish that fits into your slow cooker without touching the sides. Butter it.

2. Break eggs into buttered dish, being careful not to break the yolks. Salt and pepper.

3. Place dish on jar lid or ring or trivet in slow cooker.

4. Cover and cook on High until whites are set and yolks are as firm as you like them, about 2 hours.

5. Wearing oven gloves to protect your knuckles, remove hot dish from cooker. Gently cut eggs apart into 4 servings, and serve immediately.

Variations:

Sprinkle with grated cheese in Step 2. Place a few fresh spinach leaves on top in Step 2. The spinach will wilt by the end of cooking.

- Calories 97
- Fat 8
- Sodium 71
- Carbs 0
- Sugar 0
- Protein 6

Appetizers

Slow-Cooked Salsa

Andy Wagner, Quarryville, PA

Makes 2 cups

Prep. Time: 15 minutes   Cooking Time: 2½–3 hours
Standing Time: 2 hours   Ideal slow-cooker size: 3-qt.

10 plum tomatoes
2 cloves garlic
1 small onion, cut into wedges
1–2 jalapeño peppers
½ cup chopped fresh cilantro
½ tsp. sea salt, *optional*

1. Core tomatoes. Cut a small slit in two tomatoes. Insert a garlic clove into each slit.

2. Place all tomatoes and onion in a 3-qt. slow cooker.

3. Cut stems off jalapeños. (Remove seeds if you want a milder salsa.) Place jalapeños in the slow cooker.

4. Cover and cook on High for 2½–3 hours or until vegetables are softened. Some may brown slightly. Cool at least 2 hours with the lid off.

5. In a blender, combine the tomato mixture, cilantro, and salt if you wish. Cover and process until blended.

6. Refrigerate leftovers.

Serving suggestion:
Garnish with cilantro and jalapeño. Serve with bell pepper strips.

TIP
Wear disposable gloves when cutting hot peppers; the oils can burn your skin. Avoid touching your face when you've been working with hot peppers.

- Calories 17
- Fat 0
- Sodium 101
- Carbs 4
- Sugar 2
- Protein 1

French Onion Dip

Hope Comerford, Clinton Township, MI

Makes 6 servings
Prep. Time: 10 minutes ❧ Cooking Time: 8 hours ❧ Ideal slow-cooker size: 2-qt.

2 large sweet yellow onions, finely chopped

4 Tbsp. olive oil

1 ½ cups plain Greek yogurt

2 cloves garlic, minced

2 tsp. liquid aminos

¼ tsp. salt

¼ tsp. black pepper

Pinch of cayenne

1. Place onions and olive oil in the crock and stir so onions are coated in the olive oil.

2. Cover and cook on Low for 8 hours, or until the onions are a deep caramel brown color.

3. Strain the onions.

4. In a bowl, combine the yogurt, garlic, liquid aminos, salt, pepper, cayenne, and onions.

Serving suggestion:
Serve with crispy baked veggie chips.

- Calories 131
- Fat 9
- Sodium 121
- Carbs 6
- Sugar 4
- Protein 6

White Queso Dip

Janie Steele, Moore, OK

Makes 10–12 servings
Prep Time: 10–15 minutes ⚜ Cooking Time: 1 hour ⚜ Ideal slow-cooker size: 2-qt.

2 (8-oz.) pkgs. cream cheese, softened

1 cup sour cream

½ tsp. Frank's RedHot

10-oz. can Rotel tomatoes, your choice of hot or mild

1 tsp. cumin

4-oz. can green chilies, chopped

8-oz. pkg. grated Monterey Jack cheese, or grated Mexican cheese mix

1. Combine cream cheese, sour cream, and hot sauce in a bowl with a mixer until smooth.

2. Drain half the liquid off the tomatoes and discard.

3. Add tomatoes with half their juice, cumin, chilies, and grated cheese to creamy mixture. Stir to combine.

4. Pour mixture into slow cooker.

5. Turn to High until cheese melts, about 1 hour. Stir about every 15 minutes.

6. Turn to Low to keep dip warm while serving.

Serving suggestion:
Serve with baked, crispy cauliflower or keto chips.

- Calories 242
- Fat 22
- Sodium 341
- Carbs 5
- Sugar 3
- Protein 8

Garlicky Spinach Artichoke Dip

Hope Comerford, Clinton Township, MI

Makes 6–8 servings
Prep. Time: 10 minutes ⚘ Cooking Time: 4 hours ⚘ Ideal slow-cooker size: 3-qt.

9 oz. frozen chopped spinach, thawed, drained

14-oz. can quartered artichoke hearts, drained

½ cup plain Greek yogurt

4 oz. cream cheese, room temperature

8 cloves garlic, minced

1 cup shredded mozzarella cheese

½ cup shredded Parmesan cheese

¼ tsp. black pepper

½ tsp. kosher salt

1. Spray crock with nonstick spray.

2. Place all ingredients into crock and stir to combine well.

3. Cover and cook on Low for 4 hours.

Serving suggestion

Serve with strips of bell peppers or keto-friendly toast or crackers.

- Calories 121
- Fat 7
- Sodium 394
- Carbs 7
- Sugar 2
- Protein 9

Bacon Cheddar Dip

Arlene Snyder, Millerstown, PA

Makes 15 servings

Prep. Time: 10–15 minutes ⚜ *Cooking Time: 1½–2 hours* ⚜ *Ideal slow-cooker size: 4-qt.*

2 (8-oz.) pkgs. cream cheese, softened

2 cups sour cream

1 lb. bacon, fried and crumbled

4 cups shredded cheddar cheese, *divided*

1. In a mixing bowl, beat cream cheese and sour cream until smooth.

2. Fold in bacon and 3 cups cheddar cheese.

3. Place mixture in slow cooker and sprinkle with remaining cheese.

4. Cover and cook on Low 1½–2 hours, or until heated through.

Serving suggestion:

Serve with veggies or keto-friendly chips.

TIPS

1. Save a few bacon crumbs to sprinkle on top.

2. For a spicier version, stir in some fresh herbs, or some chopped chilies, in Step 2.

- Calories 419
- Fat 36
- Sodium 808
- Carbs 4
- Sugar 2
- Protein 20

Buffalo Chicken Dip

Amy Troyer, Garden Gove, IA

Makes 4–5 servings
Prep. Time: 10 minutes ⚒ *Cooking Time: 2–3 hours* ⚒ *Ideal slow-cooker size: 2-qt.*

8-oz. pkg. cream cheese

I cup keto-friendly blue cheese
or ranch dressing

½ cup Frank's RedHot

I cup mozzarella cheese, or your
favorite cheese

2 cups cooked and shredded chicken

1. Combine all ingredients in slow cooker.

2. Cover and cook on Low for 2–3 hours.

Serving suggestion:
Serve with keto protein pretzel sticks or cauliflower or bell pepper slices for dipping.

- Calories 563
- Fat 50
- Sodium 1238
- Carbs 5
- Sugar 4
- Protein 25

Seafood Dip

Joan Rosenberger, Stephens City, VA

Makes 24 servings of 2 Tbsp. each
Prep. Time: 5–10 minutes   &   Cooking Time: 3 hours   &   Ideal slow-cooker size: 3½-qt.

10-oz. pkg. cream cheese
6-oz. can lump crabmeat
2 Tbsp. onion, finely chopped
4–5 drops Frank's RedHot
¼ cup walnuts, finely chopped
1 tsp. paprika

1. Blend all ingredients except nuts and paprika until well mixed.

2. Spread in slow cooker. Sprinkle with nuts and paprika.

3. Cook on Low 3 hours.

Serving suggestion:
Serve with slices of keto French bread or stuff this dip inside celery sticks or serve alongside celery and bell pepper slices.

- Calories 55
- Fat 5
- Sodium 75
- Carbs 1
- Sugar 0.5
- Protein 2

Zesty Pizza Dip

Hope Comerford, Clinton Township, MI

Makes 14 servings
Prep. Time: 15 minutes & Cooking Time: 5–6 hours & Ideal slow-cooker size: 3½- or 4-qt.

1 lb. bulk turkey sausage
⅔ cup chopped onion
4 cloves garlic, minced
2 (15-oz.) cans low-sodium tomato sauce
14.5-oz. can diced tomatoes
6-oz. can low-sodium tomato paste
1 Tbsp. dried oregano
1 Tbsp. dried basil
¾ tsp. crushed red pepper
7 drops liquid stevia
½ cup sliced black olives

1. In a large skillet, brown the turkey sausage, onion, and garlic. Drain the grease.

2. In the crock, combine all the ingredients except the olives.

3. Cover and cook on Low for 5–6 hours. Just before serving, stir in the olives.

Serving suggestion:
Serve with a rainbow of bell pepper slices to dip with. Garnish with microgreens or chopped parsley.

- Calories 115
- Fat 5
- Sodium 753
- Carbs 10
- Sugar 4
- Protein 7

Crab Spread

Jeanette Oberholtzer, Manheim, PA

Makes 8 servings

Prep. Time: 20 minutes ⚬ *Cooking Time: 4 hours* ⚬ *Ideal slow-cooker size: 1- to 3-qt.*

½ cup mayonnaise

8 oz. cream cheese, softened

2 Tbsp. water

3–4 drops liquid stevia

1 onion, minced

1 lb. lump crabmeat, picked over to remove cartilage and shell bits

1. Mix mayonnaise, cheese, water, and stevia in medium-sized bowl until blended.

2. Stir in onion, mixing well. Gently stir in crabmeat.

3. Place in slow cooker, cover, and cook on Low for 4 hours.

4. Dip will hold for 2 hours. Stir occasionally.

Serving suggestion:

Serve with keto crackers or sliced veggies.

- Calories 237
- Fat 21
- Sodium 437
- Carbs 3
- Sugar 1.5
- Protein 11

Pesto Tomato Spread

Nanci Keatley, Salem, OR

Makes 12 servings
Prep. Time: 20 minutes   Cooking Time: 2–3 hours   Ideal slow-cooker size: 2-qt.

2 (8-oz.) pkgs. cream cheese, room temperature

⅔ cup prepared pesto

3 medium tomatoes, chopped

½ cup sliced black olives

½ cup chopped fresh basil

1 cup shredded mozzarella

½ cup grated Parmesan

1. Place cream cheese in bottom of lightly greased slow cooker. Push gently to make an even layer.

2. Layer rest of ingredients on top in order given.

3. Cover and cook on Low for 2–3 hours until cheese is melted and spread is hot throughout.

4. Serve as a spread on keto crackers or thin slices of keto bread or toast.

Serving suggestion:
Serve with keto bread or stuffed into celery sticks, or dipped with bell pepper slices.

- Calories 239
- Fat 22
- Sodium 407
- Carbs 5
- Sugar 3
- Protein 6

Jalapeño Poppers

Amanda Gross, Souderton, PA

Makes 10 servings
Prep. Time: 10 minutes ⚬ *Cooking Time: 2–3 hours* ⚬ *Ideal slow-cooker size: 5½-qt.*

10 medium jalapeños
4 oz. cream cheese, room temperature
¼ cup sour cream, room temperature
9 slices bacon, cooked and crumbled
¼ tsp. garlic salt
⅓ cup water

1. Cut off the tops and remove seeds and membranes to hollow out jalapeños.

2. In a bowl, mix together cream cheese, sour cream, bacon, and garlic salt.

3. Gently stuff cheese mixture into peppers.

4. Put water in the bottom of the slow cooker. Place peppers on top.

5. Cover and cook on High 2–3 hours, until peppers look slightly wrinkly and wilted.

TIP
Wear gloves to prepare the jalapeños if you are sensitive to the burning oils in hot peppers.

- Calories 45
- Fat 2.5
- Sodium 152
- Carbs 2
- Sugar 1
- Protein 4

Chicken Lettuce Wraps

Hope Comerford, Clinton Township, MI

Makes About 12 wraps

Prep. Time: 15 minutes & Cooking Time: 2–3 hours & Ideal slow-cooker size: 5- or 7-qt.

2 lb. ground chicken, browned

4 cloves garlic, minced

½ cup minced sweet yellow onion

4 Tbsp. liquid aminos

1 Tbsp. natural crunchy peanut butter (make sure it's no sugar added)

1 tsp. rice wine vinegar

1 tsp. sesame oil

¼ tsp. kosher salt

¼ tsp. red pepper flakes

¼ tsp. black pepper

3 green onions, sliced

8-oz. can sliced water chestnuts, drained, rinsed, chopped

12 good-sized pieces of iceberg lettuce, rinsed and patted dry

1. In the crock, combine the ground chicken, garlic, yellow onion, liquid aminos, peanut butter, vinegar, sesame oil, salt, red pepper flakes, and black pepper.

2. Cover and cook on Low for 2–3 hours.

3. Add in the water chestnuts and green onions. Cover and cook for an additional 10–15 minutes.

4. Serve a good spoonful on each piece of iceberg lettuce.

Serving suggestion:
Garnish with diced red bell pepper and diced green onion.

- Calories 143
- Fat 7
- Sodium 312
- Carbs 6
- Sugar 1.5
- Protein 15

Roasted Pepper and Artichoke Spread

Sherril Bieberly, Salina, KS

Makes 3 cups, or about 12 servings

Prep. Time: 10 minutes ❧ Cooking Time: 1 hour ❧ Ideal slow-cooker size: 1- to 1½-qt.

I cup grated Parmesan cheese

½ cup mayonnaise

8-oz. pkg. cream cheese, softened

I clove garlic, minced

14-oz. can artichoke hearts, drained and chopped finely

⅓ cup finely chopped roasted red bell peppers (from 7¼-oz. jar)

1. Combine Parmesan cheese, mayonnaise, cream cheese, and garlic in food processor. Process until smooth. Place mixture in slow cooker.

2. Add artichoke hearts and roasted peppers. Stir well.

3. Cover. Cook on Low 1 hour. Stir again.

Serving suggestion:

Serve as a spread for fresh, cut-up vegetables, or with keto crackers.

- Calories 162
- Fat 15
- Sodium 242
- Carbs 3
- Sugar 1
- Protein 3

Artichokes

Susan Yoder Graber, Eureka, IL

Makes 4 servings
Prep. Time: 10 minutes ♣ Cooking Time: 2–10 hours ♣ Ideal slow-cooker size: 4-qt.

4 artichokes
1 tsp. sea salt
2 Tbsp. lemon juice

1. Wash and trim artichokes by cutting off the stems flush with the bottoms of the artichokes and by cutting ¾–1 inch off the tops. Stand upright in slow cooker.

2. Mix together salt and lemon juice and pour over artichokes. Pour in water to cover ¾ of artichokes.

3. Cover. Cook on Low 8–10 hours or on High 2–4 hours.

Serving suggestion:

Serve with melted butter. Pull off individual leaves and dip bottom of each into butter. Strip the individual leaf of the meaty portion at the bottom of each leaf.

- Calories 61
- Fat 0
- Sodium 600
- Carbs 14
- Sugar 1
- Protein 4

Chili Peanuts

Hope Comerford, Clinton Township, MI

Makes 5 cups nuts
Prep. Time: 5 minutes ⚘ *Cooking Time: 2¼–2¾ hours* ⚘ *Ideal slow-cooker size: 3-qt.*

¼ cup melted butter

2 (12-oz.) cans unsalted peanuts

2 tsp. chili powder

½ tsp. ground cumin

½ tsp. paprika

½ tsp sea salt

½ tsp. dried oregano

½ tsp. garlic powder

⅛ tsp. black pepper

⅛ tsp. cayenne pepper

1. Pour butter over nuts in slow cooker.

2. Mix together all of the spices and sprinkle over the nuts in the slow cooker. Toss together.

3. Cover. Cook on Low 2–2½ hours. Turn to High. Remove lid and cook 10–15 minutes.

- Calories 225
- Fat 19
- Sodium 42
- Carbs 7
- Sugar 1
- Protein 8

Curried Almonds

Barbara Aston, Ashdown, AR

Makes 4 cups

Prep. Time: 5 minutes & Cooking Time: 3–4½ hours & Ideal slow-cooker size: 3-qt.

¼ cup butter

I Tbsp. curry powder

½ tsp. sea salt

⅛ tsp. turmeric

⅛ tsp. paprika

⅛ tsp. onion powder

⅛ tsp. garlic powder

I drop liquid stevia

I lb. blanched almonds

1. Combine butter with curry powder, sea salt, turmeric, paprika, onion powder, garlic powder, and liquid stevia.

2. Pour over almonds in slow cooker. Mix to coat well.

3. Cover. Cook on Low 2–3 hours. Turn to High. Uncover cooker and cook 1–1½ hours.

4. Serve warm or at room temperature.

- Calories 359
- Fat 31
- Sodium 44
- Carbs 12
- Sugar 2
- Protein 13

Bacon Spinach Dip

Amy Bauer, New Ulm, MN

Makes 8–10 servings
Prep. Time: 15 minutes ❧ Cooking Time: 2 hours ❧ Ideal slow-cooker size: 3-qt.

½ lb. bacon, diced

1 lb. cheddar cheese, shredded

8-oz. pkg. cream cheese, room temperature

10-oz. pkg. frozen chopped spinach, thawed and drained

14½-oz. can Rotel tomatoes and green chilies, undrained

1. Fry bacon in skillet until crisp. Remove bacon and set aside on a paper towel. Transfer bacon drippings to slow cooker.

2. Add rest of ingredients (except bacon pieces) and stir.

3. Cover and cook on Low 2 hours, or until cheese is melted.

4. Just before serving, stir in the bacon pieces.

Serving suggestion:

Serve with carrot and celery sticks.

- Calories 384
- Fat 31
- Sodium 947
- Carbs 6
- Sugar 2
- Protein 21

Soups, Stews & Chilies

Broccoli-Cheese Soup

Hope Comerford, Clinton Township, MI

Makes 8 servings
Prep. Time: 20 minutes & Cooking Time: 8–10 hours & Ideal slow-cooker size: 4-qt.

2 (16-oz.) pkgs. frozen chopped broccoli

2¾ cups heavy cream

12-oz. can evaporated milk

½ cup chicken bone broth

¼ cup finely chopped onion

2 Tbsp. butter

1 Tbsp. Italian seasoning

¼ tsp. onion powder

¼ tsp. pepper

2 cups cheddar cheese

1. Combine all ingredients in the crock except the cheddar cheese and stir to combine.

2. Cover. Cook on Low 8–10 hours.

3. Stir in the cheese and let cook another hour, stirring every 20 minutes or so.

- Calories 365
- Fat 32
- Sodium 280
- Carbs 10
- Sugar 5
- Protein 13

Onion Soup

Lucille Amos, Greensboro, NC

Makes 10 servings

Prep. Time: 30 minutes ❧ *Cooking Time: 4–5 hours* ❧ *Ideal slow-cooker size: 4- to 5-qt.*

6 large onions

1 stick (8 Tbsp.) butter

8 cups beef bone broth

1½ tsp. liquid aminos

Pepper, to taste

Shredded mozzarella cheese and Parmesan cheese, *optional*

1. In large skillet or saucepan, sauté onions in butter until tender. Do not brown. Transfer to slow cooker.

2. Add broth, liquid aminos, and pepper.

3. Cover. Cook on Low 4–5 hours or until onions are very tender.

4. Top each serving with cheese.

- Calories 222
- Fat 10
- Sodium 655
- Carbs 26
- Sugar 6
- Protein 8

Tomato Basil Soup

Janet Melvin, Cincinnati, OH

Makes 12 servings
Prep. Time: 15 minutes ⚜ *Cooking Time: 3½ hours* ⚜ *Ideal slow-cooker size: 4-qt.*

½ cup very finely diced onion

2 cloves garlic, minced

2 cups low-sodium vegetable stock

2 (28-oz.) cans crushed tomatoes

¼ cup chopped fresh basil, plus more for garnish

1 Tbsp. salt

½ tsp. pepper

1 cup heavy cream, room temperature

1. Combine onion, garlic, stock, tomatoes, basil, salt, and pepper in slow cooker.

2. Cover and cook on High for 3 hours. May puree soup at this point if you wish for a totally smooth soup.

3. Stir in heavy cream and cook an additional 30 minutes on Low.

4. Garnish each serving with a few ribbons of fresh basil.

- Calories 115
- Fat 7
- Sodium 743
- Carbs 11
- Sugar 6
- Protein 11

Cabbage Soup

Margaret Jarrett, Anderson, IN

Makes 8 servings
Prep. Time: 25 minutes ⚬ Cooking Time: 3½–4 hours ⚬ Ideal slow cooker size: 4-qt.

Half a head of cabbage, sliced thin

2 ribs celery, sliced thin

½ cup chopped cauliflower

1 carrot, sliced

14-oz. can diced tomatoes

1 onion, chopped

2 cups chicken bone broth

2 cloves garlic, minced

1 qt. unsalted tomato juice (make sure it has no added sugar)

¼ tsp. pepper

Water

1. Combine all ingredients except water in slow cooker. Add water to within 3 inches of top of slow cooker.

2. Cover. Cook on High 3½–4 hours, or until vegetables are tender.

- Calories 53
- Fat 1
- Sodium 498
- Carbs 9
- Sugar 4.5
- Protein 3

Slow-Cooker Loaded Cauliflower Soup

Hope Comerford, Clinton Township, MI

Makes 8–10 servings
Prep. Time: 15 minutes ☙ Cooking Time: 6 hours ☙ Ideal slow-cooker size: 5-qt.

32 oz. chicken bone broth

2 cups heavy cream

2 heads cauliflower, chopped

1 small onion, chopped

2 cloves garlic, minced

¼ tsp. pepper

1. Place all ingredients into crock. Stir until combined.

2. Cover and cook on Low for 6 hours.

3. With an immersion blender or a potato masher, mash any remaining chunks in your soup.

Serving suggestion:

Top with shredded cheese, cooked chopped bacon, and chopped green onions.

- Calories 190
- Fat 18
- Sodium 172
- Carbs 4
- Sugar 2.5
- Protein 4

Shredded Pork Soup

Hope Comerford, Clinton Township, MI

Makes 6–8 servings
Prep. Time: 10 minutes ♣ *Cooking Time: 8–10 hours* ♣ *Ideal slow-cooker size: 5-qt.*

3 large tomatoes, chopped

I cup chopped red onion

I jalapeño, seeded and minced

1-lb. pork loin

2 tsp. cumin

2 tsp. chili powder

2 tsp. onion powder

2 tsp. garlic powder

2 tsp. lime juice

8 cups chicken bone broth

Garnish (*optional*):

Fresh chopped cilantro

Avocado slices

Freshly grated Mexican cheese

1. In your crock, place the tomatoes, onion, and jalapeños.

2. Place the pork loin on top.

3. Add all the seasonings and lime juice, and pour in the chicken broth.

4. Cover and cook on Low for 8–10 hours.

5. Remove the pork and shred it between two forks. Place it back into the soup and stir.

6. Serve each bowl of soup with fresh chopped cilantro, avocado slices, and freshly grated Mexican cheese, if desired . . . or any other garnishes you would like!

TIP
If you don't have time for freshly chopped tomatoes, use a can of diced or chopped tomatoes.

- Calories 145
- Fat 5
- Sodium 787
- Carbs 6
- Sugar 3
- Protein 18

Taco Soup

Hope Comerford, Clinton Township, MI

Makes 4–6 servings
Prep. Time: 20 minutes ⚓ Cooking Time: 8 hours ⚓ Ideal slow-cooker size: 4-qt.

2 lb. ground turkey

I large onion, chopped

2 tsp. chili powder

2 tsp. garlic powder

I tsp. dried parsley

I tsp. onion powder

½ tsp. ground cumin

½ tsp. paprika

½ tsp. dried dill

2 tsp. sea salt

½ tsp. dried oregano

¼ tsp. black pepper

⅛ tsp. cayenne pepper

2 (14½-oz.) cans diced tomatoes

4 cups beef bone broth

1. Brown turkey meat with the onion.

2. Place the browned meat into the crock and add all the remaining ingredients. Stir.

3. Cover and cook on Low for 8 hours.

Serving suggestion:
Serve with sour cream, shredded cheese, and chunks of avocado.

- Calories 217
- Fat 1
- Sodium 1353
- Carbs 10
- Sugar 2
- Protein 40

Ham and Green Bean Soup

Loretta Krahn, Mountain Lake, MN

Makes 6 servings
Prep. Time: 20 minutes ♣ Cooking Time: 4–6 hours ♣ Ideal slow-cooker size: 4-qt.

1 meaty ham bone
1½ qts. water
1 large onion, chopped
3 cups chopped green beans
2 celery stalks, chopped
1 cup chopped cauliflower
1 Tbsp. parsley
1 Tbsp. summer savory
¼ tsp. pepper
1 cup heavy cream

1. Combine all ingredients except heavy cream in slow cooker.

2. Cover. Cook on High 4–6 hours.

3. Remove ham bone. Cut off meat and return to slow cooker.

4. Turn to Low. Stir in cream or milk. Heat through and serve.

- Calories 150
- Fat 8
- Sodium 25
- Carbs 8
- Sugar 3
- Protein 2.1

Sausage, Tomato, and Spinach Soup

Wendy B. Martzall, New Holland, PA

Makes 8 servings
Prep. Time: 15–20 minutes ⚘ *Cooking Time: 5 hours* ⚘ *Ideal slow-cooker size: 3- to 4-qt.*

½ lb. loose pork or turkey sausage

1 medium onion, chopped

1 small green bell pepper, chopped

28-oz. can diced tomatoes

4 cups beef bone broth

8-oz. can no-salt-added tomato sauce

2 tsp. Frank's RedHot

7 drops liquid stevia

1 tsp. dried basil

½ tsp. dried oregano

10-oz. pkg. frozen spinach, thawed and squeezed dry

½ cup shredded mozzarella cheese

1. Brown sausage with onions and peppers in skillet. (If you use turkey sausage, you'll probably need to add 1–2 Tbsp. oil to the pan.) Stir frequently, breaking up clumps of meat. When no longer pink, drain off drippings.

2. Spoon meat and vegetables into slow cooker.

3. Add all remaining ingredients except spinach and cheese. Stir until well blended.

4. Cover. Cook on Low 4¾ hours.

5. Stir spinach into soup. Cover and continue cooking on Low another 15 minutes.

6. Top each individual serving with a sprinkling of mozzarella cheese.

- Calories 150
- Fat 5.5
- Sodium 946
- Carbs 11
- Sugar 3
- Protein 12

Cabbage and Beef Soup

Colleen Heatwole, Burton, MI

Makes 6–8 servings
Prep. Time: 20 minutes ⚜ *Cooking Time: 6–8 hours* ⚜ *Ideal slow-cooker size: 5-qt.*

1 lb. ground beef

1 can tomatoes, 28–32 oz., or 1 quart home-canned tomatoes

½ tsp. garlic salt

¼ tsp. onion powder

¼ tsp. garlic powder

¼ tsp. pepper

2 ribs celery, chopped

½ medium head cabbage, chopped

4 cups beef bone broth

Chopped fresh parsley, for garnish

1. Brown beef in large skillet. Add tomatoes and chop coarsely. Transfer to slow cooker.

2. Add remaining ingredients, except parsley.

3. Cover and cook 6–8 hours on Low.

4. Serve in bowls garnished with fresh parsley.

- Calories 127
- Fat **5**
- Sodium 458
- Carbs 6
- Sugar 4
- Protein 15

Sausage and Cabbage Soup

Donna Suter, Pandora, OH

Makes 6–8 servings
Prep. Time: 20 minutes ⚬ Cooking Time: 6–8 hours ⚬ Ideal slow-cooker size: 4-qt.

1 lb. Bob Evans sausage

4 cups vegetable broth

2 cups chicken bone broth

1 onion, chopped

½ head cabbage, chopped

4–6 ribs celery, sliced

14-oz. can diced tomatoes

4 cloves garlic, chopped

2 tsp. dried basil

1 tsp. salt

½ tsp. pepper

1. Brown sausage in skillet and drain off grease. Transfer sausage to slow cooker.

2. Add rest of ingredients to slow cooker.

3. Cover and cook on Low for 6–8 hours.

- Calories 207
- Fat 16
- Sodium 1085
- Carbs 7.5
- Sugar 4
- Protein 8

Stuffed Pepper Soup

Shelia Heil, Lancaster, PA

Makes 8–10 servings
Prep. Time: 45 minutes ☙ *Cooking Time: 3–4 hours* ☙ *Ideal slow-cooker size: 6-qt.*

1 lb. ground beef
1 small onion, diced
1 large green bell pepper, diced
1 large red bell pepper, diced
26-oz. can diced tomatoes
8-oz. can tomato sauce
2 cups beef bone broth
15 drops liquid stevia
1 tsp. garlic powder
Salt and pepper, to taste

1. In a large skillet, brown beef, cutting into small pieces as it browns.

2. Add peppers and onion and fry briefly. Drain off drippings. Transfer mixture to slow cooker.

3. Add rest of ingredients. Stir.

4. Cover and cook on Low 3–4 hours, to meld flavors.

- Calories 148
- Fat 9
- Sodium 381
- Carbs 6
- Sugar 2
- Protein 9

Zucchini Stew

Colleen Heatwole, Burton, MI

Makes 6 servings
Prep. Time: 30 minutes ⚜ *Cooking Time: 4–6 hours* ⚜ *Ideal slow-cooker size: 6-qt.*

I lb. bulk Italian sausage

2 ribs of celery, diced

2 medium green bell peppers, diced

I medium onion, chopped

2 (28-oz.) cans of diced tomatoes

2 lb. zucchini, cut into ½-inch slices

2 cloves garlic, minced

5 drops liquid stevia

I tsp. oregano

I tsp. Italian seasoning

I tsp. salt, *optional* (taste first)

6 Tbsp. grated Parmesan cheese

1. Brown sausage in hot skillet until brown and crumbly, about 5–7 minutes. Drain and discard grease.

2. Mix celery, bell peppers, and onion into cooked sausage and cook and stir until they are softened, 10–12 minutes.

3. Combine remaining ingredients, except Parmesan cheese, and add to slow cooker.

4. Cook on Low 4–6 hours. Garnish each serving with 1 Tbsp. Parmesan cheese.

- Calories 250
- Fat 9
- Sodium 1045
- Carbs 24
- Sugar 8
- Protein 19

Colorful Beef Stew

Hope Comerford, Clinton Township, MI

Makes 6 servings
Prep. Time: 20 minutes ⚜ Cooking Time: 8–9 hours ⚜ Ideal slow-cooker size: 4-qt.

2-lb. boneless beef chuck roast, trimmed of fat and cut into ¾-inch pieces

1 large red onion, chopped

2 cups beef bone broth

6-oz. can tomato paste

4 cloves garlic, minced

1 Tbsp. paprika

2 tsp. dried marjoram

½ tsp. black pepper

1 tsp. sea salt

1 red bell pepper, sliced

1 yellow bell pepper, sliced

1 orange bell pepper, sliced

1. Place all ingredients in the crock except the sliced bell peppers, and stir.

2. Cover and cook on Low for 8–9 hours. Stir in sliced bell peppers the last 45 minutes of cooking time.

- Calories 361
- Fat 22
- Sodium 643
- Carbs 11
- Sugar 5
- Protein 32

Pungent Beef Stew

Grace Ketcham, Marietta, GA

Makes 4–6 servings
Prep. Time: 15 minutes & Cooking Time: 10–12 hours & Ideal slow-cooker size: 4½-qt.

2 lb. beef chuck, cubed

8-oz. can tomato sauce

1 tsp. liquid aminos

1 clove garlic, minced

1 medium onion, chopped

2 bay leaves

½ tsp. salt

½ tsp. paprika

¼ tsp. pepper

Dash of ground cloves, or allspice

14-oz. can diced tomatoes

1 cup chopped green beans

2 cups chopped cauliflower

2 ribs celery, chopped

½ cup water

1. Combine all ingredients in slow cooker.

2. Cover. Cook on Low 10–12 hours.

- Calories 261
- Fat 11
- Sodium 433
- Carbs 9
- Sugar 3
- Protein 33

Meatball Stew

Barbara Hershey, Lititz, PA

Makes 8 servings
Prep Time: 1 hour (includes preparing and baking meatballs)   *Cooking Time: 4–5 hours*
Ideal slow-cooker size: 4- or 6-qt.

Meatballs

2 lb. 90%-lean ground beef

2 eggs, beaten

2 Tbsp. dried onion

½ tsp. salt

¼ tsp. pepper

1 tsp. Dijon mustard

2 tsp. liquid aminos

4 cups chopped cauliflower

1 large onion, sliced

2 cups chopped broccoli

4 cups no-sugar-added tomato juice

1 tsp. dried basil

1 tsp. dried oregano

½ tsp. pepper

Salt, to taste

1. In a bowl, thoroughly mix meatball ingredients together. Form into 1-inch balls.

2. Place meatballs on a lightly greased rimmed baking sheet. Bake at 400°F for 20 minutes.

3. Meanwhile, place all vegetables in slow cooker.

4. When finished baking, remove meatballs from pan.

5. Place meatballs on top of vegetables in slow cooker.

6. In a large bowl, combine tomato juice and seasonings. Pour over meatballs and vegetables in slow cooker.

7. Cover. Cook on High 4–5 hours, or until vegetables are tender.

- Calories 253
- Fat 13
- Sodium 343
- Carbs 7
- Sugar 3
- Protein 26

Santa Fe Stew

Jeanne Allen, Rye, CO

Makes 4–6 servings
Prep. Time: 20 minutes ⚶ Cooking Time: 8 hours ⚶ Ideal slow-cooker size: 4-qt.

2 lb. sirloin, or stewing meat, cubed

1 large onion, diced

2 cloves garlic, minced

2 Tbsp. olive oil

3 cups beef bone broth

1 Tbsp. dried parsley flakes

1 tsp. ground cumin

½ tsp. salt

3 zucchini squash, diced

14½-oz. can diced tomatoes

14½-oz. can green beans, drained, or
1 lb. frozen green beans

4-oz. can diced green chilies

1. Brown meat, onion, and garlic in oil in saucepan. Place in slow cooker.

2. Stir in remaining ingredients.

3. Cover. Cook on Low for 8 hours.

- Calories 334
- Fat 18
- Sodium 305
- Carbs 9
- Sugar 4
- Protein 35

Chicken Chili

Sharon Miller, Holmesville, OH

Makes 6 servings
Prep. Time: 15 minutes ☙ Cooking Time: 5–6 hours ☙ Ideal slow-cooker size: 4-qt.

2 lb. boneless, skinless chicken breasts, cubed

2 Tbsp. butter

2 (14-oz.) cans diced tomatoes, undrained, *divided*

1 cup diced onion

1 cup diced red bell pepper

1–2 Tbsp. chili powder, according to your taste preference

1 tsp. ground cumin

1 tsp. ground oregano

Salt and pepper, to taste

1. In skillet on high heat, brown chicken cubes in butter until they have some browned edges. Place in greased slow cooker.

2. Pour one of the cans of tomatoes with its juice into skillet to get all the browned bits and butter. Scrape and pour into slow cooker.

3. Add rest of ingredients, including other can of tomatoes, to cooker.

4. Cook on Low for 5–6 hours.

Serving suggestion:
Can be served with shredded cheddar cheese, sour cream, and avocado slices.

- Calories 253
- Fat 7
- Sodium 335
- Carbs 11
- Sugar 3
- Protein 35

Pork Chili

Carol Duree, Salina, KS

Makes 5 servings
Prep. Time: 15 minutes ❧ Cooking Time: 4–8 hours ❧ Ideal slow cooker size: 4-qt.

I lb. boneless pork ribs
2 (14½-oz.) cans diced tomatoes
4¼-oz. can diced green chili peppers, drained
½ cup chopped onion
I clove garlic, minced
I Tbsp. chili powder

1. Layer ingredients into slow cooker in order given.

2. Cover. Cook on High 4 hours or on Low 6–8 hours, or until pork is tender but not dry.

3. Cut up or shred meat. Stir through chili and serve.

- Calories 280
- Fat 15
- Sodium 368
- Carbs 11
- Sugar 3
- Protein 25

White Chicken Chili

Jewel Showalter, Landisville, PA

Makes 6–8 servings
Prep. Time: 25 minutes ⚬ Cooking Time: 7 hours ⚬ Ideal slow-cooker size: 5-qt.

2 whole skinless chicken breasts

6 cups water

2 onions, chopped

2 cloves garlic, minced

1 Tbsp. olive oil

2–4 (4¼-oz.) cans chopped green chilies, drained, depending on your taste preference

1–2 diced jalapeño peppers

2 tsp. ground cumin

1½ tsp. dried oregano

¼ tsp. cayenne pepper

½ tsp. salt

1–2 cups shredded cheese

Sour cream

Salsa

Avocado chunks

1. Place all ingredients except the cheese, sour cream, salsa, and avocado chunks into crock.

2. Cover. Cook on Low 7 hours.

3. Remove chicken from slow cooker and cube it. Place it back into the crock. Stir in the cheese.

4. Serve topped with cheese, sour cream, salsa, and avocado chunks.

- Calories 238
- Fat 10
- Sodium 267
- Carbs 7
- Sugar 3
- Protein 30

No-Beans Chili

Sharon Timpe, Jackson, WI

Makes 10–12 servings

Prep. Time: 35 minutes ❧ Cooking Time: Low 9–10 hours; High 6–7 hours ❧ Ideal slow-cooker size: 5- or 6-qt.

2–3 Tbsp. olive oil
1½ lb. round steak, cubed
1½ lb. chuck steak, cubed
2 cups beef bone broth
1½ tsp. dried oregano
2 tsp. dried parsley
1 medium onion, chopped
1 cup chopped celery
1 cup diced bell peppers
28-oz. can stewed tomatoes
8-oz. can tomato sauce
1 Tbsp. vinegar
1½ tsp. Truvia brown sugar blend
2 Tbsp. chili powder
1 tsp. cumin
¼ tsp. pepper
1 tsp. salt

1. Heat oil in a skillet and brown the beef cubes. You may have to do this in two batches.

2. Put browned beef in slow cooker.

3. Add the beef bone broth to skillet and stir, scraping up browned bits. Scrape/pour mixture into slow cooker.

4. Add rest of ingredients to slow cooker.

5. Cook on Low 9–10 hours or High 6–7 hours, until meat is very tender.

Serving suggestion:
Serve in bowls garnished with toppings like grated cheese, sour cream, blue cheese crumbles, and avocado chunks.

- Calories 258
- Fat 11
- Sodium 728
- Carbs 13
- Sugar 4
- Protein 27

Our Favorite Chili

Ruth Shank, Gridley, IL

Makes 10–12 servings
Prep. Time: 20 minutes & Cooking Time: 4–10 hours & Ideal slow-cooker size: 5-qt.

3 lb. ground beef
¼ cup chopped onions
I rib celery, chopped
I Tbsp. olive oil
29-oz. can stewed tomatoes
½ cup tomato sauce
1½ tsp. lemon juice
2 tsp. vinegar
¾ tsp. Truvia brown sugar blend
1½ tsp. salt
I tsp. liquid aminos
½ tsp. garlic powder
½ tsp. dry mustard powder
I Tbsp. chili powder
2 (6-oz.) cans tomato paste

1. Brown ground beef, onions, and celery in skillet in oil. Stir frequently to break up clumps of meat. When meat is no longer pink, drain off drippings.

2. Place meat and vegetables in slow cooker. Add all remaining ingredients. Mix well.

3. Cover. Cook on Low 8–10 hours or on High 4–5 hours.

Serving suggestion:

Top with diced avocado and sprinkled with Colby or Monterey Jack cheese.

- Calories 231
- Fat 13
- Sodium 901
- Carbs 16
- Sugar 6
- Protein 13

Hearty Chili

Joylynn Keener, Lancaster, PA

Makes 8 servings
Prep. Time: 20–25 minutes ⚮ Cooking Time: 8 hours ⚮ Ideal slow-cooker size: 5-qt.

I onion, chopped
2 ribs celery, chopped
3 lb. ground beef
I Tbsp. olive oil
14-oz. can diced tomatoes
2 (14-oz.) cans tomato sauce
I green bell pepper, chopped
15 drops liquid stevia
I tsp. salt
I tsp. dried thyme
I tsp. dried oregano
I Tbsp. chili powder, or to taste

1. Brown onion, celery, and beef in skillet in oil if needed. Stir frequently to break up clumps of meat. When meat is no longer pink, drain off drippings.

2. Spoon meat into slow cooker. Stir in all remaining ingredients, mixing well.

3. Cover. Cook on Low 8 hours.

- Calories 205
- Fat 13
- Sodium 847
- Carbs 10
- Sugar 8
- Protein 12

Texican Chili

Becky Oswald, Broadway, VA

Makes 15 servings
Prep. Time: 20 minutes ❧ *Cooking Time: 9–10 hours* ❧ *Ideal slow-cooker size: 5- to 6-qt.*

8 bacon strips, diced

2½ lb. beef stewing meat, cubed

28-oz. can stewed tomatoes

14½-oz. can stewed tomatoes

2 (8-oz.) cans tomato sauce

1 medium onion, chopped

1 cup chopped celery

2 cups chopped bell pepper (any color(s))

¼ cup minced fresh parsley

1 Tbsp. chili powder

1 tsp. salt

½ tsp. ground cumin

¼ tsp. pepper

1. Cook bacon in skillet until crisp. Drain on paper towel.

2. Brown beef in bacon drippings in skillet.

3. Combine all ingredients in slow cooker.

4. Cover. Cook on Low 9–10 hours, or until meat is tender. Stir occasionally.

- Calories 212
- Fat 11
- Sodium 723
- Carbs 7
- Sugar 4
- Protein 22

Chili Con Carne

Donna Conto, Saylorsburg, PA

Makes 4–6 servings
Prep. Time: 15 minutes ⚘ Cooking Time: 5–6 hours ⚘ Ideal slow-cooker size: 4-qt.

1½ lb. ground beef
1 cup chopped onions
¾ cup chopped green peppers
1 clove garlic, minced
14½-oz. can chopped tomatoes
8-oz. can tomato sauce
2 tsp. chili powder
½ tsp. dried basil

1. Brown beef, onions, green pepper, and garlic in saucepan. Drain.

2. Combine all ingredients in slow cooker.

3. Cover. Cook on Low 5–6 hours.

- Calories 326
- Fat 23
- Sodium 372
- Carbs 9
- Sugar 5
- Protein 21

Dorthea's Slow-Cooker Chili

Dorothea K. Ladd, Ballston Lake, NY

Makes 6–8 servings
Prep. Time: 15 minutes & Cooking Time: 8–10 hours & Ideal slow-cooker size: 6½-qt.

1 lb. ground beef
1 lb. bulk pork sausage
1 large onion, chopped
1 large green pepper, chopped
1 large red pepper, chopped
2–3 ribs celery, chopped
29-oz. can tomato purée
6-oz. can tomato paste
2 cloves garlic, minced
2 Tbsp. chili powder
2 tsp. salt

1. Brown ground beef and sausage in skillet. Drain.

2. Combine all ingredients in slow cooker.

3. Cover. Cook on Low 8–10 hours.

Serving suggestion:
Top individual servings with shredded sharp cheddar cheese.

Variations:

1. For extra flavor, add 1 tsp. cayenne pepper.

2. For more zest, use mild or hot Italian sausage instead of regular pork sausage.

- Calories 394
- Fat 28
- Sodium 1435
- Carbs 16
- Sugar 9
- Protein 19

Gumbo

Dorothy Ealy, Los Angeles, CA

Makes 8 servings

Prep. Time: 30 minutes ❧ *Cooking Time: 4½–5½ hours* ❧ *Ideal slow-cooker size: 5-qt.*

2 onions, chopped

3 ribs celery, chopped

½ cup diced green bell pepper

2 cloves garlic, chopped

1 cup chopped fresh or frozen okra

½ cup diced andouille or chorizo sausage

2 (15-oz.) cans tomatoes, undrained

3 Tbsp. tomato paste

1 chicken bouillon cube

¼ tsp. freshly ground black pepper

¼ tsp. dried thyme

1½ lb. raw shrimp, peeled and deveined, chopped if large

1. In slow cooker, combine onions, celery, bell pepper, garlic, okra, sausage, tomatoes, tomato paste, bouillon cube, black pepper, and thyme.

2. Cover and cook on Low for 4–5 hours, until vegetables are soft.

3. Add shrimp. Cook for 15–20 more minutes on Low, until shrimp are just opaque and cooked through. Thin gumbo if necessary with a little water, broth, or wine. Taste and adjust salt.

Serving suggestion:

Pass the hot sauce so people can make it really authentically spicy!

NOTE

If you are peeling the shrimp yourself, save the shells. Place them in a saucepan with water or chicken broth just to cover and simmer for 30 minutes. Strain out shells and discard. This makes a tasty seafood-infused broth for making other soups or thinning the gumbo.

- Calories 132
- Fat 5
- Sodium 837
- Carbs 10
- Sugar 4
- Protein 16

Oceanside Bisque

Jane Geigley, Lancaster, PA

Makes 8 servings
Prep. Time: 30 minutes   ⚜   Cooking Time: 2–3 hours   ⚜   Ideal slow-cooker size: 6-qt.

1 Tbsp. unsalted butter

1 Tbsp. olive oil

3 large shallots, minced (or 1 medium-sized Vidalia onion, minced)

5½ cups chicken bone broth

2 cups heavy cream

1 Tbsp. kosher salt

½ tsp. freshly ground white pepper

1 lb. fresh or thawed lump crabmeat (picked over for shell fragments), or canned crabmeat

Fresh tarragon or flat-leaf parsley for garnish

1. In small saucepan, melt butter and oil over medium heat.

2. Add shallots and sauté until translucent (about 2–3 minutes).

3. Pour into slow cooker.

4. Add broth and cream.

5. Season with salt and pepper.

6. Cook on High for ½ hour.

7. Add crabmeat.

8. Stir.

9. Cook for another 2–3 hours.

10. Ladle into bowls and garnish with tarragon or parsley.

Serving suggestion:

This is also delicious with fresh chopped parsley on top and a sprinkle of turmeric or paprika.

- Calories 334
- Fat 27
- Sodium 1232
- Carbs 8
- Sugar 5
- Protein 15

Main Dishes

Chicken & Turkey

Garlic and Lemon Chicken

Hope Comerford, Clinton Township, MI

Makes 5 servings
Prep. Time: 5 minutes & Cooking Time: 5–6 hours & Ideal slow-cooker size: 3- or 5-qt.

4–5 lb. boneless skinless chicken breasts or thighs

½ cup minced shallots

½ cup olive oil

¼ cup lemon juice

1 Tbsp. garlic paste (or use 1 medium clove garlic, minced)

1 Tbsp. no-salt seasoning

⅛ tsp. pepper

1. Place chicken in slow cooker.

2. In a small bowl, mix the remaining ingredients. Pour this mixture over the chicken in the crock.

3. Cover and cook on Low for 5–6 hours.

- Calories 641
- Fat 32
- Sodium 165
- Carbs 4
- Sugar 1.5
- Protein 82

Bacon-Feta Stuffed Chicken

Tina Goss, Duenweg, MO

Makes 4 servings
Prep. Time: 10 minutes ❧ *Cooking Time: 1½–3 hours* ❧ *Ideal slow-cooker size: 3-qt.*

¼ cup crumbled cooked bacon

¼ cup crumbled feta cheese

4 boneless, skinless chicken breast halves

2 (14½-oz.) cans diced tomatoes

1 Tbsp. dried basil

1. In a small bowl, mix bacon and cheese together lightly.

2. Cut a pocket in the thicker side of each chicken breast. Fill each with ¼ of the bacon and cheese. Pinch shut and secure with toothpicks.

3. Place chicken in slow cooker. Top with tomatoes and sprinkle with basil.

4. Cover and cook on High 1½–3 hours, or until chicken is tender, but not dry or mushy.

- Calories 437
- Fat 14
- Sodium 857
- Carbs 11
- Sugar 2
- Protein 61

Ann's Chicken Cacciatore

Ann Driscoll, Albuquerque, NM

Makes 6–8 servings
Prep. Time: 10 minutes   &   Cooking Time: 3–9 hours   &   Ideal slow-cooker size: 4-qt.

1 large onion, thinly sliced

2½–3-lb. chicken, cut up

2 (6-oz.) cans tomato paste

4-oz. sliced mushrooms

1 tsp. salt

¼ cup chicken bone broth

¼ tsp. pepper

1–2 cloves garlic, minced

1–2 tsp. dried oregano

½ tsp. dried basil

½ tsp. celery seed, *optional*

1 bay leaf

1. Place onion in slow cooker. Add chicken.

2. Combine remaining ingredients. Pour over chicken.

3. Cover. Cook on Low 7–9 hours, or on High 3–4 hours.

- Calories 217
- Fat 4
- Sodium 703
- Carbs 10
- Sugar 6
- Protein 34

Darla's Chicken Cacciatore

Darla Sathre, Baxter, MN

Makes 6 servings
Prep. Time: 5–10 minutes ❧ *Cooking Time: 8 hours* ❧ *Ideal slow-cooker size: 4-qt.*

2 onions, thinly sliced
4 boneless chicken breasts, cubed
3 cloves garlic, minced
¼ tsp. pepper
2 tsp. dried oregano
1 tsp. dried basil
1 bay leaf
2 (15-oz.) cans diced tomatoes
8-oz. can tomato sauce
4-oz. can sliced mushrooms

1. Place onions in bottom of slow cooker. Add remaining ingredients.

2. Cover. Cook on Low 8 hours.

- Calories 246
- Fat 4
- Sodium 372
- Carbs 11
- Sugar 2
- Protein 37

Chicken Dijon Dinner

Barbara Stutzman, Crossville, TN

Makes 4–6 servings
Prep. Time: 20 minutes   ❧   Cooking Time: 4 hours   ❧   Ideal slow-cooker size: 6-qt.

2 lb. boneless, skinless chicken thighs
2 cloves garlic, minced
1 Tbsp. olive oil
6 Tbsp. white wine vinegar
4 Tbsp. liquid aminos
4 Tbsp. Dijon mustard
1 lb. sliced mushrooms

1. Grease interior of slow-cooker crock.

2. Place thighs in crock. If you need to add a second layer, stagger the pieces so they don't directly overlap each other.

3. Stir together garlic, oil, vinegar, liquid aminos, and mustard until well mixed.

4. Gently stir in mushrooms.

5. Spoon sauce into crock, making sure to cover all thighs with some of the sauce.

6. Cover. Cook on Low for 4 hours, or until instant-read meat thermometer registers 160°F when stuck in center of chicken.

7. Serve chicken topped with sauce.

- Calories 218
- Fat 10
- Sodium 803
- Carbs 1
- Sugar 0
- Protein 30

Tarragon Chicken

Cassius L. Chapman, Tucker, GA

Makes 6 servings
Prep. Time: 15–20 minutes & Cooking Time: 4 hours & Ideal slow-cooker size: 5-qt.

6 boneless, skinless chicken thighs

½ tsp. salt

½ tsp. coarsely ground black pepper

1 tsp. dried tarragon

2 Tbsp. chopped onion

½ cup chicken bone broth

2 Tbsp. butter

2 Tbsp. flaxseed

¼ tsp. salt

1 cup heavy cream

1 Tbsp. chopped fresh tarragon

1. Grease interior of slow-cooker crock.

2. Place thighs in cooker. If you need to create a second layer, stagger the pieces so they don't directly overlap each other.

3. In a small bowl, mix together salt, pepper, dried tarragon, chopped onion, and broth.

4. Spoon over thighs, making sure to top those on both levels with the sauce.

5. Cover. Cook on Low for 4 hours, or until instant-read meat thermometer registers 160°–165°F when stuck in the thighs.

6. Close to end of cooking time, melt butter in skillet or small saucepan. Blend in flaxseed and salt. Cook, stirring continuously over heat for 1–2 minutes until all clumps are broken up.

7. Gradually pour in cream, stirring continuously over medium heat until sauce thickens.

8. To serve, place thighs on platter. Spoon sauce over. Sprinkle with chopped fresh tarragon leaves.

- Calories 296
- Fat 22
- Sodium 349
- Carbs 2
- Sugar 1
- Protein 16

Butter Chicken

Pat Bishop, Bedminster, PA

Makes 8 servings

Prep. Time: 20 minutes ❧ *Cooking Time: 4¼ hours* ❧ *Ideal slow-cooker size: 5- to 6-qt.*

2 onions, diced

3 cloves garlic, minced

3 Tbsp. butter, softened to room temperature

2 Tbsp. grated fresh ginger

1 Tbsp. Truvia brown sugar blend

2 tsp. chili powder

¾ tsp. ground coriander

¾ tsp. turmeric

½ tsp. ground cinnamon

½ tsp. ground cumin

½ tsp. salt

¼ tsp. black pepper

28-oz. can diced tomatoes, undrained

1 cup chicken bone broth

¼ cup natural peanut butter, almond butter, or cashew butter (no sugar added)

3 lb. boneless, skinless chicken thighs, halved

1 cup sour cream

2 Tbsp. chopped fresh cilantro

- Calories 394
- Fat 18
- Sodium 464
- Carbs 13
- Sugar 5
- Protein 42

1. Grease interior of slow-cooker crock.

2. In crock combine onions, garlic, butter, fresh ginger, brown sugar, chili powder, coriander, turmeric, cinnamon, cumin, salt, pepper, and tomatoes.

3. In a bowl, whisk broth with nut butter. Pour into crock. Stir everything together until well blended.

4. Settle chicken thighs into sauce, submerging as much as possible.

5. Cover. Cook on Low for 4 hours, or until instant-read meat thermometer registers 160°F when stuck in center of thigh pieces.

6. Remove chicken with slotted spoon and place in bowl. Cover and keep warm.

7. With immersion blender, puree sauce until smooth. Add chicken back into sauce.

8. Cover. Cook another 15 minutes, or until heated through.

9. Stir in sour cream.

10. Serve sprinkled with cilantro.

Southwestern Shredded Chicken

Hope Comerford, Clinton Township, MI

Makes 4 servings
Prep. Time: 8–10 minutes & Cooking Time: 5–6 hours & Ideal slow-cooker size: 3-qt.

1 ½ lb. boneless, skinless chicken breast
1 Tbsp. chili powder
2 tsp. garlic powder
1 tsp. cumin
1 tsp. onion powder
½ tsp. kosher salt
¼ tsp. pepper
1 medium onion, chopped
14.5-oz. can diced tomatoes
4-oz. can diced green chilies
½ cup sour cream

1. Place the chicken in the slow cooker.

2. Mix together the chili powder, garlic powder, cumin, onion powder, kosher salt, and pepper. Sprinkle this over both sides of the chicken.

3. Sprinkle the onion over the top of the chicken and pour the can of diced tomatoes and green chilies over the top.

4. Cover and cook on Low for 5–6 hours.

5. Turn your slow cooker to warm. Remove the chicken and shred it between 2 forks.

6. Slowly whisk in the sour cream with the juices in the crock. Replace the chicken in the crock and stir to mix in the juices.

Serving suggestion:
Serve topped with some shredded lettuce, shredded cheese, and fresh salsa.

- Calories 309
- Fat 10
- Sodium 547
- Carbs 13
- Sugar 4
- Protein 41

Szechuan-Style Chicken and Broccoli

Jane Meiser, Harrisonburg, VA

Makes 4 servings
Prep. Time: 30 minutes ❧ *Cooking Time: 1½–3 hours* ❧ *Ideal slow-cooker size: 4-qt.*

2 whole boneless, skinless chicken breasts

I Tbsp. olive oil

½ cup chicken bone broth

10 drops Frank's RedHot

2 Tbsp. liquid aminos

2 drops liquid stevia

2 tsp. flaxseed

I medium onion, chopped

2 cloves garlic, minced

½ tsp. ground ginger

2 cups broccoli florets

I medium red bell pepper, sliced

1. Cut chicken into 1-inch cubes and brown lightly in oil in skillet. Place in slow cooker.

2. Stir in remaining ingredients.

3. Cover. Cook on High 1–1½ hours or on Low 2–3 hours.

- Calories 219
- Fat 7
- Sodium 171
- Carbs 8
- Sugar 3
- Protein 29

Savory Slow-Cooker Chicken

Sara Harter Fredette, Williamsburg, MA

Makes 4 servings
Prep. Time: 25 minutes ⚜ *Cooking Time: 8–10 hours* ⚜ *Ideal slow-cooker size: 4- or 5-qt.*

2½ lb. chicken pieces, skinned

1 lb. fresh tomatoes, chopped, or 15-oz. can stewed tomatoes

1 bay leaf

¼ tsp. pepper

2 cloves garlic, minced

1 onion, chopped

½ cup chicken bone broth

1 tsp. dried thyme

¼ tsp. salt

2 cups broccoli, cut into bite-sized pieces

1. Combine all ingredients except broccoli in slow cooker.

2. Cover. Cook on Low 8–10 hours.

3. Add broccoli 30 minutes before serving.

- Calories 401
- Fat 8
- Sodium 312
- Carbs 11
- Sugar 5
- Protein 67

Traditional Turkey Breast

Hope Comerford, Clinton Township, MI

Makes 10–12 servings
Prep. Time: 10 minutes & Cooking Time: 8 hours & Ideal slow-cooker size: 7-qt.

7-lb. or less turkey breast

Olive oil

½ stick butter, 8 pieces

Rub:

2 tsp. garlic powder

1 tsp. onion powder

1 tsp. salt

¼ tsp. pepper

1 tsp. poultry seasoning (make sure this has no sugar added to it)

1. Remove the gizzards from the turkey breast, rinse it, and pat dry. Place the breast into the crock.

2. Rub the turkey breast all over with olive oil.

3. Mix together all the rub ingredients. Rub this all over the turkey breast and press it in.

4. Place the pieces of butter all over the top of the breast.

5. Cover and cook on Low for 8 hours.

Serving suggestion:
Serve with mashed cauliflower and keto stuffing.

- Calories 326
- Fat 5
- Sodium 1981
- Carbs 5
- Sugar 0
- Protein 51

Pork

Garlic Pork Roast in the Slow-cooker

Earnie Zimmerman, Mechanicsburg, PA

Makes 10 servings

Prep. Time: 15–20 minutes ⚜ *Cooking Time: 4–5 hours* ⚜ *Ideal slow-cooker size: 6- to 8-qt.*

3-lb. boneless pork loin roast, short and wide rather than long and narrow

1 Tbsp. butter

1 tsp. salt

½ tsp. coarsely ground black pepper

1 medium onion, sliced

6 cloves garlic, peeled

8 strips (each 3 inches long, ½ inch wide) fresh lemon peel

1 head cauliflower, broken up

1 lb. celery sticks

½ tsp. dried thyme

1 cup chicken bone broth

1. Grease interior of slow-cooker crock.

2. If you have time, heat butter in 12-inch skillet over medium-high heat until hot. Place pork roast in skillet and brown on all sides. Move meat to crock.

3. If you don't have time, place pork in crock directly.

4. Sprinkle all over with salt and pepper.

5. In a large bowl, mix together onion, garlic, lemon peel, cauliflower, celery, and thyme. Stir in chicken broth.

6. Spoon mixture into crock alongside meat and over top.

7. Cover. Cook on Low 4 hours, or until instant-read meat thermometer registers 140°–145°F when stuck in center of roast. Remove roast to cutting board. Cover to keep warm. Let stand for 10 minutes.

8. Check if onions, potatoes, and carrots are as tender as you like them. If not, cover crock and continue cooking another 30–60 minutes, or until veggies are as done as you want.

9. Slice pork into ½-inch-thick slices. Place on deep platter. Serve topped with vegetables and broth.

- Calories 352
- Fat 19
- Sodium 381
- Carbs 5
- Sugar 2
- Protein 38

Savory Pork Roast

Mary Louise Martin, Boyd, WI

Makes 4–6 servings
Prep. Time: 15 minutes ❧ Cooking Time: 3½–4½ hours ❧ Ideal slow-cooker size: oval 6-qt.

4 lb. boneless pork butt roast
1 tsp. ground ginger
1 Tbsp. fresh minced rosemary
½ tsp. mace or nutmeg
1 tsp. coarsely ground black pepper
2 tsp. salt
2 cups water

1. Grease interior of slow cooker crock.

2. Place roast in slow cooker.

3. In a bowl, mix spices and seasonings together. Sprinkle half on top of roast, pushing down on spices to encourage them to stick.

4. Flip roast and sprinkle with rest of spices, again, pushing down to make them stick.

5. Pour 2 cups water around the edge, being careful not to wash spices off meat.

6. Cover. Cook on Low 3½–4½ hours, or until instant-read meat thermometer registers 140°F when stuck into center of roast.

- Calories 513
- Fat 34
- Sodium 1111
- Carbs 1
- Sugar 0
- Protein 52

Barbara Jean's Whole Pork Tenderloin

Barbara Jean Fabel, Wausau, WI

Makes 8 servings
Prep. Time: 20 minutes ✧ Cooking Time: 3–5 hours ✧ Ideal slow-cooker size: 4- or 5-qt.

½ cup sliced celery

¼ lb. fresh mushrooms, quartered

1 medium onion, sliced

3 Tbsp. butter, *divided*

2 (1¼-lb.) pork tenderloins, trimmed of fat

1 Tbsp. olive oil

½ cup beef bone broth

¾ tsp. salt

¼ tsp. pepper

1 Tbsp. flaxseed

1. Placed celery, mushrooms, onion, and 2 Tbsp. butter in slow cooker.

2. Brown tenderloins in skillet in 1 Tbsp. olive oil. Layer over vegetables in slow cooker.

3. Pour beef broth over tenderloins. Sprinkle with salt and pepper.

4. Combine 1 Tbsp. butter and flaxseed until smooth. Pour over tenderloins.

5. Cover. Cook on High 3 hours or Low 4–5 hours.

- Calories 227
- Fat 11
- Sodium 414
- Carbs 2
- Sugar 1
- Protein 30

Pork Tenderloin with Mustard Sauce

Bobbie Jean Weidner Muscarella, State College, PA

Makes 10–12 servings
Prep. Time: 20 minutes ♣ Cooking Time: 3–4 hours
Marinating Time: 2–3 hours ♣ Ideal slow-cooker size: oval 6- or 7-qt.

Roast Pork:
½ cup liquid aminos

½ cup beef bone broth

⅛ cup Truvia brown sugar blend

3-lb. boneless pork loin roast (wide and short; not skinny and long)

Mustard Sauce:
1 Tbsp. dry mustard

¼ cup Dijon mustard

30 drops liquid stevia

½ tsp. salt

2 Tbsp. apple cider vinegar

4 egg yolks, beaten

1 cup cream

TIP
You can make the Mustard Sauce ahead of time and keep it in the fridge for up to 3 days. The sauce is also delicious on ham.

- Calories 232
- Fat 13
- Sodium 939
- Carbs 3
- Sugar 3
- Protein 26

1. Grease interior of slow-cooker crock.

2. In a bowl, mix together liquid aminos, beef bone broth, and brown sugar blend.

3. Place pork in bowl. Pour marinade over it. Cover.

4. Marinate at room temperature for 2–3 hours, turning meat over occasionally.

5. Place meat in crock. Pour marinade over top.

6. Cover. Cook on Low 3–4 hours, or until instant-read meat thermometer registers 140°–145°F when stuck into center.

7. While roast is cooking, place dry mustard, Dijon mustard, liquid stevia, salt, vinegar, and egg yolks in top of double boiler.

8. Cook over simmering water, stirring constantly until thickened.

9. Cool slightly. Then stir in cream. Set aside. (You can serve it at room temperature or heated slightly.)

10. Lift roast out of cooker with sturdy tongs or 2 sturdy metal spatulas onto cutting board. Cover and keep warm. Let stand 10 minutes.

11. Slice into thin, diagonal slices and serve with mustard sauce.

Pork and Cabbage Dinner

Mrs. Paul Gray, Beatrice, NE

Makes 8 servings
Prep. Time: 25 minutes ☙ Cooking Time: 5–6 hours ☙ Ideal slow cooker size: 4- or 5-qt.

2 lb. pork steaks, or chops, or shoulder, bone in, trimmed of fat

¾ cup chopped onions

¼ cup chopped fresh parsley, or 2 Tbsp. dried parsley

4 cups shredded cabbage

1 tsp. salt

⅛ tsp. pepper

½ tsp. caraway seeds

⅛ tsp. allspice

½ cup beef bone broth

1. Place pork in slow cooker. Layer onions, parsley, and cabbage over pork.

2. Combine salt, pepper, caraway seeds, and allspice. Sprinkle over cabbage. Pour broth over cabbage.

3. Cover. Cook on Low 5–6 hours.

- Calories 156
- Fat 4
- Sodium 381
- Carbs 4
- Sugar 2
- Protein 28

Teriyaki Pork Steak with Sugar Snap Peas

Hope Comerford, Clinton Township, MI

Makes 4–6 servings
Prep. Time: 10 minutes ⚮ Cooking Time: 7–9 hours ⚮ Ideal slow-cooker size: 5-qt.

2½-lb. pork shoulder blade steaks

I Tbsp. onion powder, *divided*

I Tbsp. garlic powder, *divided*

Salt and pepper, to taste

I cup liquid aminos

15 drops liquid stevia

½ Tbsp. flaxseed

½ medium onion, sliced into half rings

1½–2 cups sugar snap peas

1. Place the pork steaks in your crock and sprinkle them with half the onion powder, garlic powder, and a bit of salt and pepper.

2. Mix together the liquid aminos, liquid stevia, and flaxseed.

3. Pour half of the liquid aminos sauce over the contents of the crock.

4. Place your onions on top and sprinkle them with more salt, pepper, and the rest of the garlic powder and onion powder. Pour the rest of the liquid aminos sauce over the top.

5. Cover and cook on Low for 7–9 hours.

6. About 40 minutes before the cook time is up, add in the sugar snap peas.

7. Serve the pork with some of the sugar snap peas on top and sauce from the crock drizzled over the top.

- Calories 440
- Fat 29
- Sodium 1875
- Carbs 5
- Sugar 2
- Protein 43

Spicy Pork Chops

Mary Puskar, Forest Hill, MD

Makes 5 servings
Prep. Time: 15 minutes ❧ *Cooking Time: 6–8 hours* ❧ *Ideal slow-cooker size: 4-qt.*

5–6 center-cut loin pork chops
3 Tbsp. olive oil
I onion, sliced
I green pepper, cut in strips
8-oz. can tomato sauce
1½ Tbsp. Truvia brown sugar blend
I Tbsp. vinegar
1½ tsp. salt
I tsp. liquid aminos

1. Brown chops in oil in skillet. Transfer to slow cooker.

2. Add remaining ingredients to cooker.

3. Cover. Cook on Low 6–8 hours.

Serving suggestion:
Delicious with mashed cauliflower.

- Calories 215
- Fat 11
- Sodium 910
- Carbs 8
- Sugar 6
- Protein 21

Beef

Corned Beef

Margaret Jarrett, Anderson, IN

Makes 6–7 servings
Prep. Time: 5 minutes ♣ Cooking Time: 4–5 hours ♣ Ideal slow-cooker size: 5-qt.

2–3-lb. cut of marinated corned beef

2–3 cloves garlic, minced

10–12 peppercorns

1. Place meat in bottom of cooker. Top with garlic and peppercorns. Cover with water.

2. Cover. Cook on High 4–5 hours, or until tender.

- Calories 326
- Fat 25
- Sodium 1261
- Carbs 1
- Sugar 0
- Protein 24

Four-Pepper Steak

Renee Hankins, Narvon, PA

Makes 14 servings
Prep. Time: 30 minutes ⚜ *Cooking Time: 5–8 hours* ⚜ *Ideal slow-cooker size: 4- or 5-qt.*

1 yellow pepper, sliced into ¼-inch-thick pieces

1 red pepper, sliced into ¼-inch-thick pieces

1 orange pepper, sliced into ¼-inch-thick pieces

1 green pepper, sliced into ¼-inch thick-pieces

2 cloves garlic, sliced

2 large onions, sliced

1 tsp. ground cumin

½ tsp. dried oregano

1 bay leaf

3 lb. flank steak, cut in ¼–½-inch thick slices across the grain

Salt, to taste

2 (14.5-oz.) cans low-sodium diced tomatoes in juice

Jalapeño chilies, sliced, *optional*

1. Place sliced bell peppers, garlic, onions, cumin, oregano, and bay leaf in slow cooker. Stir gently to mix.

2. Put steak slices on top of vegetable mixture. Season with salt.

3. Spoon tomatoes with juice over top. Sprinkle with jalapeño pepper slices if you wish. Do not stir.

4. Cover and cook on Low 5–8 hours, depending on your slow cooker. Check after 5 hours to see if meat is tender. If not, continue cooking until tender but not dry.

- Calories 191
- Fat 8
- Sodium 160
- Carbs 7
- Sugar 2
- Protein 22

Corned Beef and Cabbage

Rhoda Burgoon, Collingswood, NJ
Jo Ellen Moore, Pendleton, IN

Makes 6–8 servings
Prep. Time: 5 minutes ✤ Cooking Time: 7–13 hours ✤ Ideal slow-cooker size: 5- to 6-qt.

½ head cauliflower, broken into pieces

3–4-lb. corned beef brisket

2–3 medium onions, quartered

¾–1¼ cups water

Half a small head of cabbage, cut in wedges

1. Layer all ingredients, except cabbage, in slow cooker.

2. Cover. Cook on Low 8–10 hours, or on High 5–6 hours.

3. Add cabbage wedges to liquid, pushing down to moisten. Turn to High and cook an additional 2–3 hours.

Serving suggestion:

Top individual servings with mixture of sour cream and horseradish.

—Kathi Rogge, Alexandria, IN

NOTE

To cook more cabbage than slow cooker will hold, cook separately in skillet. Remove 1 cup broth from slow cooker during last hour of cooking. Pour over cabbage wedges in skillet. Cover and cook slowly for 20–30 minutes.

- Calories 466
- Fat 34
- Sodium 2774
- Carbs 5
- Sugar 4
- Protein 34

Herbed Pot Roast

Sarah Herr, Goshen, IN

Makes 6 servings
Prep. Time: 20 minutes & Cooking Time: 6–8 hours on Low & Ideal slow-cooker size: oval 6-qt.

2 lb. boneless beef chuck roast

½ head cauliflower, broken/chopped into pieces

2 cups Brussels sprouts

2 ribs celery, cut into small chunks

½ tsp. salt

½ tsp. dried rosemary

½ tsp. dried thyme

¼ tsp. garlic powder

¼ tsp. onion powder

¼ tsp. paprika

¼ tsp. coarsely ground pepper

3 Tbsp. balsamic vinegar

1. Grease interior of slow-cooker crock.

2. Place roast in crock.

3. Place veggies around roast.

4. Sprinkle herbs and spices evenly over all.

5. Drizzle balsamic vinegar over top.

6. Cover. Cook on Low 6–8 hours.

- Calories 234
- Fat 9
- Sodium 312
- Carbs 5
- Sugar 2
- Protein 33

Marinated Chuck Roast

Susan Nafziger, Canton, KS

Makes 7–8 servings
Prep. Time: 15 minutes ⚓ *Cooking Time: 5-6 hours*
Marinating Time: 2–3 hours ⚓ *Ideal slow-cooker size: oval 5-qt.*

1 cup olive oil

1 cup liquid aminos

¼ cup red wine vinegar

½ cup chopped onions

⅛ tsp. garlic powder

¼ tsp. ground ginger

½ tsp. black pepper (coarsely ground is best)

½ tsp. dry mustard

3–4-lb. boneless chuck roast

1. Mix all ingredients except chuck roast, either by whisking together in a bowl or whirring the mixture in a blender.

2. Place roast in a low baking or serving dish and pour marinade over top. Cover and refrigerate for 2–3 hours.

3. Grease interior of slow-cooker crock.

4. Place roast in crock. Pour marinade over top.

5. Cover. Cook on Low 5–6 hours, or until instant-read meat thermometer registers 140°–145°F when stuck into center of meat.

6. When finished cooking, use a sturdy pair of tongs, or 2 metal spatulas, to move roast onto a cutting board. Cover to keep warm and allow to stand 15 minutes.

7. Cut into slices or chunks. Top with marinade and serve.

- Calories 551
- Fat 47
- Sodium 1464
- Carbs 2
- Sugar 0
- Protein 36

Spicy Beef Roast

Karen Ceneviva, Seymour, CT

Makes 10 servings
Prep. Time: 15–20 minutes & Cooking Time: 3–8 hours & Ideal slow-cooker size: 4- or 5-qt.

3-lb. eye of round roast, trimmed of fat
1–2 Tbsp. cracked black peppercorns
2 cloves garlic, minced
3 Tbsp. balsamic vinegar
⅓ cup liquid aminos
2 tsp. dry mustard

1. Rub cracked pepper and garlic onto roast. Put roast in slow cooker.

2. Make several shallow slits in top of meat.

3. In a small bowl, combine remaining ingredients. Spoon over meat.

4. Cover and cook on Low for 6–8 hours, or on High for 3–4 hours, just until meat is tender, but not dry.

- Calories 177
- Fat 4
- Sodium 423
- Carbs 2
- Sugar 1
- Protein 33

Hungarian Beef with Paprika

Maureen Csikasz, Wakefield, MA

Makes 9 servings
Prep. Time: 15 minutes ❧ *Cooking Time: 3–6 hours* ❧ *Ideal slow-cooker size: oval 5- or 6-qt.*

3-lb. boneless chuck roast

2–3 medium onions, coarsely chopped

5 Tbsp. sweet paprika

¾ tsp. salt

¼ tsp. black pepper

½ tsp. caraway seeds

I clove garlic, chopped

½ green bell pepper, sliced

¼ cup water

½ cup sour cream

fresh parsley

1. Grease interior of slow cooker crock.

2. Place roast in crock.

3. In a good-sized bowl, mix all ingredients together, except sour cream and parsley.

4. Spoon evenly over roast.

5. Cover. Cook on High 3–4 hours, or on Low 5–6 hours, or until instant-read meat thermometer registers 140–145°F when stuck in center of meat.

6. When finished cooking, use sturdy tongs or 2 metal spatulas to lift meat to cutting board. Cover with foil to keep warm. Let stand 10–15 minutes.

7. Cut into chunks or slices.

8. Just before serving, dollop with sour cream. Garnish with fresh parsley.

- Calories 312
- Fat 20
- Sodium 289
- Carbs 4
- Sugar 2
- Protein 30

Carol's Italian Beef

Carol Findling, Princeton, IL

Makes 6–8 servings
Prep. Time: 5–10 minutes ♣ *Cooking Time: 4–12 hours* ♣ *Ideal slow-cooker size: 4-qt.*

3–4-lb. lean rump roast

2 tsp. salt, *divided*

4 cloves garlic

2 tsp. Romano, or Parmesan, cheese, *divided*

1 ½ cup beef bone broth

1 tsp. dried oregano

1. Place roast in slow cooker. Cut 4 slits in top of roast. Fill each slit with ½ tsp. salt, 1 garlic clove, and ½ tsp. cheese.

2. Pour broth over meat. Sprinkle with oregano.

3. Cover. Cook on Low 10–12 hours, or on High 4–6 hours.

4. Remove meat and slice or shred.

- Calories 246
- Fat 11
- Sodium 713
- Carbs 1
- Sugar 0
- Protein 40

Slow-Cooked Pepper Steak

Carolyn Baer, Conrath, WI
Ann Driscoll, Albuquerque, NM

Makes 8 servings
Prep. Time: 25 minutes ❧ *Cooking Time: 6–7 hours* ❧ *Ideal slow-cooker size: 4-qt.*

1½–2 lb. beef round steak, cut in 3-inch × 1-inch strips, trimmed of fat

2 Tbsp. olive oil

¼ cup liquid aminos

1 clove garlic, minced

1 cup chopped onion

5 drops liquid stevia

¼ tsp. pepper

¼ tsp. ground ginger

2 large green peppers, cut in strips

4 medium tomatoes cut in eighths, or 16-oz. can diced tomatoes

½ cup cold water

1 Tbsp. flaxseed

1. Brown beef in oil in saucepan. Transfer to slow cooker.

2. Combine liquid aminos, garlic, onion, stevia, pepper, and ginger. Pour over meat.

3. Cover. Cook on Low 5–6 hours.

4. Add green peppers and tomatoes. Cook 1 hour longer.

5. Combine water and flaxseed. Stir into slow cooker. Cook on High until thickened, about 10 minutes.

Serving suggestion:
Serve with riced cauliflower.

- Calories 213
- Fat 11
- Sodium 415
- Carbs 5
- Sugar 2
- Protein 26

Three-Pepper Steak

Renee Hankins, Narvon, PA

Makes 10 servings
Prep. Time: 15 minutes   Cooking Time: 5–8 hours   Ideal slow-cooker size: 4- or 5-qt.

3 bell peppers—one red, one orange, and one yellow pepper (or any combination of colors), cut into ¼-inch-thick slices

2 cloves garlic, sliced

1 large onion, sliced

1 tsp. ground cumin

½ tsp. dried oregano

1 bay leaf

3-lb. beef flank steak, cut in ¼–½-inch-thick slices across the grain

Salt, to taste

14½-oz. can diced tomatoes in juice

Jalapeño chilies, sliced, *optional*

1. Place sliced peppers, garlic, onion, cumin, oregano, and bay leaf in slow cooker. Stir gently to mix.

2. Put steak slices on top of vegetable mixture. Season with salt.

3. Spoon tomatoes with juice over top. Sprinkle with jalapeño pepper slices if you wish. Do not stir.

4. Cover. Cook on Low 5–8 hours, depending on your slow cooker. Check after 5 hours to see if meat is tender. If not, continue cooking until tender but not dry.

Serving suggestion:
Serve over riced cauliflower.

- Calories 260
- Fat 12
- Sodium 154
- Carbs 4
- Sugar 1
- Protein 30

Asian Pepper Steak

Donna Lantgen, Rapid City, SD

Makes 6 servings
Prep. Time: 20 minutes ⚜ *Cooking Time: 6–8 hours* ⚜ *Ideal slow-cooker size: 4-qt.*

1-lb. round steak, sliced thin, trimmed of fat

3 Tbsp. liquid aminos

½ tsp. ground ginger

1 clove garlic, minced

1 medium green pepper, thinly sliced

1 cup sliced fresh mushrooms

1 medium onion, thinly sliced

½ tsp. crushed red pepper

1. Combine all ingredients in slow cooker.

2. Cover. Cook on Low 6–8 hours.

- Calories 117
- Fat 5
- Sodium 387
- Carbs 3
- Sugar 1
- Protein 17

Slow-Cooker Sirloin Steak

Amy Troyer, Garden Grove, IA

Makes 4–5 servings
Prep. Time: 10 minutes   ♣   Cooking Time: 6–8 hours   ♣   Ideal slow-cooker size: 2- to 3-qt.

2½-lb. sirloin steak, cut into ½-inch strips
1 large onion, sliced
2 bell peppers, sliced
1 tsp. ginger
15 drops liquid stevia
2 Tbsp. olive oil
½ cup liquid aminos
2 cloves garlic, minced

1. Place steak in slow cooker, and top with the sliced onion and peppers.

2. Mix together remaining ingredients.

3. Pour sauce over meat, onions, and peppers.

4. Cook on Low 6–8 hours.

- Calories 303
- Fat 16
- Sodium 1195
- Carbs 4
- Sugar 1
- Protein 53

Nadine and Hazel's Swiss Steak

Nadine Martinitz, Salina, KS
Hazel L. Propst, Oxford, PA

Makes 6–8 servings
Prep. Time: 20 minutes ⚜ *Cooking Time: 6–8 hours* ⚜ *Ideal slow-cooker size: 6-qt.*

3-lb. round steak

⅓ cup almond flour

2 tsp. salt

½ tsp. pepper

3 Tbsp. butter

1 large onion, or more, sliced

1 large pepper, or more, sliced

14½-oz. can stewed tomatoes, or 3–4 fresh tomatoes, chopped

Water

1. Sprinkle meat with almond flour, salt, and pepper. Pound both sides. Cut into 6 or 8 pieces. Brown meat in butter over medium heat on top of stove, about 15 minutes. Transfer to slow cooker.

2. Brown onion and pepper. Add tomatoes and bring to boil. Pour over steak. Add water to completely cover steak.

3. Cover. Cook on Low 6–8 hours.

Variation:

To add some flavor, stir in your favorite dried herbs when beginning to cook the steak, or add fresh herbs in the last hour of cooking.

- Calories 349
- Fat 19
- Sodium 832
- Carbs 9
- Sugar 2
- Protein 38

Cabbage Lasagna

Sylvia Eberly, Reinholds, PA

Makes 4–5 servings
Prep. Time: 30 minutes ❧ Cooking Time: 5 hours ❧ Ideal slow-cooker size: 5-qt.

1 medium to large head cabbage, about 6 inches in diameter

1 lb. ground beef

2 cloves garlic, minced or pressed

1 medium onion, chopped

1 green sweet bell pepper, chopped

6-oz. can tomato paste

8-oz. can tomato sauce

1–3 tsp. dried oregano, according to your taste preference

2 tsp. dried basil, *optional*

1 tsp. black pepper

1 cup mozzarella cheese, grated, *divided*

½ cup ricotta or cottage cheese, *divided*

½ cup grated Parmesan cheese

- Calories 460
- Fat 27
- Sodium 880
- Carbs 24
- Sugar 13
- Protein 31

1. Wash cabbage and remove tough outer leaves. Cut head in half and slice thinly.

2. Arrange finely sliced cabbage in a steamer basket and steam about 3–5 minutes. (You might need to do this in two batches.)

3. Drain cabbage well. Set aside.

4. Grease interior of slow-cooker crock.

5. If you have time, brown beef, garlic, onion, and green pepper together in a skillet. Drain off any drippings. If you don't have time, place beef in bowl and use a sturdy spoon to break up into small clumps. Mix in garlic, onion, and green pepper.

6. Add tomato paste, tomato sauce, and seasonings to beef mixture. Combine well.

7. Drain cabbage again.

8. Make layers in crock, starting with half the cabbage leaves, half the meat mixture, ⅓ of the mozzarella, and half the ricotta.

9. Repeat layers, using remaining cabbage and meat mixture, half the remaining mozzarella, and all of the ricotta.

10. Top with remaining mozzarella.

11. Cover. Cook on Low 5 hours, or until vegetables are as tender as you like them.

12. Uncover. Sprinkle with Parmesan cheese.

13. Let stand 10 minutes so that Parmesan cheese can melt and lasagna firms up.

Zucchini and Beef Lasagna

Carolyn Snyder, Ephrata, PA

Makes 4 servings
Prep. Time: 15–20 minutes   ❧   Cooking Time: 4 hours   ❧   Ideal slow-cooker size: 4- or 5-qt.

I lb. ground beef

½ tsp. dried basil

½ tsp. dried oregano

⅛ tsp. garlic powder

6-oz. can tomato paste

I cup cottage cheese

I egg

2 cups mozzarella cheese, shredded, *divided*

6 cups sliced, unpeeled zucchini

1. Grease interior of slow-cooker crock.

2. If you have time, brown beef in a skillet. Using a slotted spoon, lift beef out of drippings and place in good-sized bowl. If you don't have time, place beef in bowl and use a sturdy spoon to break into small clumps.

3. Mix basil, oregano, and garlic powder with beef.

4. Stir tomato paste into beef mixture.

5. In a separate bowl, combine cottage cheese, egg, and 1 cup mozzarella.

6. Cover bottom of crock with half the zucchini slices.

7. Top with half the meat mixture.

8. Spoon half the cheese mixture over meat.

9. Repeat layers.

10. Cover. Cook on Low 4 hours, or until zucchini is as tender as you like.

11. Uncover crock. Sprinkle in remaining mozzarella cheese. Allow to stand 10 minutes so cheese can melt and lasagna can firm up.

- Calories 620
- Fat 40
- Sodium 1171
- Carbs 18
- Sugar 13
- Protein 50

Nutritious Meatloaf

Elsie Russett, Fairbank, IA

Makes 6 servings
Prep. Time: 10 minutes ⚘ *Cooking Time: 3–4 hours* ⚘ *Ideal slow-cooker size: 4-qt.*

1 lb. ground beef
2 cups finely shredded cabbage
1 medium green pepper, diced
1 Tbsp. dried onion flakes
½ tsp. caraway seeds
1 tsp. salt

1. Combine all ingredients. Shape into loaf and place on rack in slow cooker.

2. Cover. Cook on High 3–4 hours.

- Calories 185
- Fat 14
- Sodium 371
- Carbs 2
- Sugar 1
- Protein 14

Mexican Meatloaf

Jennifer Freed, Rockingham, VA

Makes 4–6 servings
Prep. Time: 20 minutes   ❧   *Cooking Time: 5–7 hours*   ❧   *Ideal slow-cooker size: 3- to 4-qt.*

2 lb. ground beef

2 cups ground pork rinds

1 cup shredded cheddar cheese

⅔ cup salsa

2 eggs, beaten

4 Tbsp. taco seasoning

1. Combine all ingredients in large bowl; mix well.

2. Shape meat mixture into loaf and place in slow cooker.

3. Cover; cook on Low for 5–7 hours, or until internal temperature is 165°F.

Serving suggestion:
Serve with mashed cauliflower.

- Calories 531
- Fat 38
- Sodium 1022
- Carbs 6
- Sugar 2
- Protein 40

Meatless & Seafood

Eggplant Italian

Melanie Thrower, McPherson, KS

Makes 6–8 servings
Prep. Time: 30 minutes   Cooking Time: 4 hours   Ideal slow-cooker size: oval 4- or 5-qt.

2 eggplants
1 egg
24 oz. cottage cheese
¼ tsp. salt
Black pepper, to taste
14-oz. can tomato sauce
2–4 Tbsp. Italian seasoning, according to your taste preference

1. Peel eggplants and cut in ½-inch thick slices. Soak in saltwater for about 5 minutes to remove bitterness. Drain well.

2. Spray slow cooker with cooking spray.

3. Mix egg, cottage cheese, salt, and pepper together in bowl.

4. Mix tomato sauce and Italian seasoning together in another bowl.

5. Spoon a thin layer of tomato sauce into bottom of slow cooker. Top with about one-third of eggplant slices, and then one-third of egg/cheese mixture, and finally one-third of remaining tomato sauce mixture.

6. Repeat those layers twice, ending with seasoned tomato sauce.

7. Cover. Cook on High 4 hours. Allow to rest 15 minutes before serving.

- Calories 124
- Fat 3
- Sodium 568
- Carbs 15
- Sugar 10
- Protein 12

Lemon Dijon Fish

June S. Groff, Denver, PA

Makes 4 servings
Prep. Time: 10 minutes ❧ Cooking Time: 3 hours ❧ Ideal slow-cooker size: 2-qt.

1½ lb. orange roughy fillets

2 Tbsp. Dijon mustard

3 Tbsp. butter, melted

1 tsp. liquid aminos

1 Tbsp. lemon juice

1. Cut fillets to fit in slow cooker.

2. In a bowl, mix remaining ingredients together. Pour sauce over fish. (If you have to stack the fish, spoon a portion of the sauce over the first layer of fish before adding the second layer.)

3. Cover and cook on Low 3 hours, or until fish flakes easily but is not dry or overcooked.

- Calories 305
- Fat 19
- Sodium 315
- Carbs 1
- Sugar 0
- Protein 33

Side Dishes & Vegetables

Broccoli and Bell Peppers

Frieda Weisz, Aberdeen, SD

Makes 8 servings

Prep. Time: 20 minutes ❧ *Cooking Time: 4–5 hours* ❧ *Ideal slow-cooker size: 3½- or 4-qt.*

2 lb. fresh broccoli, trimmed and chopped into bite-sized pieces

I clove garlic, minced

I green or red bell pepper, cut into thin slices

I onion, peeled and cut into slices

4 Tbsp. liquid aminos

½ tsp. salt

Dash of black pepper

I Tbsp. sesame seeds, *optional*, as garnish

1. Combine all ingredients except sesame seeds in slow cooker.

2. Cook on Low for 4–5 hours. Top with sesame seeds.

- Calories 20
- Fat 0.5
- Sodium 459
- Carbs 3.5
- Sugar 1
- Protein 2

Cheesy Broccoli Casserole

Dorothy VanDeest, Memphis, TN

Makes 3–4 servings
Prep. Time: 10–15 minutes ⚭ *Cooking Time: 3–5 hours* ⚭ *Ideal slow-cooker size: 3-qt.*

10-oz. pkg. frozen chopped broccoli

6 eggs, beaten

24 oz. small-curd cottage cheese

6 Tbsp. almond flour

8 oz. mild cheese of your choice, diced

½ stick (4 Tbsp.) butter, melted

2 green onions, chopped

Salt, to taste

1. Place frozen broccoli in colander. Run cold water over it until it thaws. Separate into pieces. Drain well.

2. Combine broccoli and all other ingredients in greased slow cooker. Mix together gently but well.

3. Cover. Cook on High 1 hour. Stir well, then continue cooking on Low 2–4 hours.

- Calories 785
- Fat 61
- Sodium 1068
- Carbs 15
- Sugar 7
- Protein 46

Julia's Broccoli and Cauliflower with Cheese

Julia Lapp, New Holland, PA

Makes 6 servings
Prep. Time: 25 minutes & Cooking Time: 1½ hours & Ideal slow-cooker size: 4-qt.

5 cups chopped broccoli and cauliflower

¼ cup water

2 Tbsp. butter

2 Tbsp. almond flour

½ tsp. salt

1 cup whole milk

1 cup shredded cheddar cheese

1. Cook broccoli and cauliflower in saucepan in water, until just crisp-tender. Set aside.

2. Make white sauce by melting the butter in another pan over low heat. Blend in flour and salt. Add milk all at once. Cook quickly, stirring constantly until mixture thickens and bubbles. Add cheese. Stir until melted and smooth.

3. Combine vegetables and sauce in slow cooker. Mix well.

4. Cook on Low 1½ hours.

- Calories 140
- Fat 9
- Sodium 326
- Carbs 8
- Sugar 3.5
- Protein 8

Doris's Broccoli and Cauliflower with Cheese

Doris G. Herr, Manheim, PA

Makes 8 servings

Prep. Time: 5 minutes & Cooking Time: 1½–3 hours & Ideal slow-cooker size: 3-qt.

1 lb. frozen cauliflower, chopped

2 (10-oz.) pkgs. frozen broccoli, chopped

½ cup water

2 cups shredded cheddar cheese

1. Place cauliflower and broccoli in slow cooker.

2. Add water. Top with cheese.

3. Cook on Low 1½–3 hours, depending upon how crunchy or soft you want the vegetables.

- Calories 154
- Fat 10
- Sodium 225
- Carbs 8
- Sugar 2
- Protein 10

Italian Vegetables

Susie Shenk Wenger, Lancaster, PA

Makes 6 servings
Prep. Time: 30 minutes ⚹ Cooking Time: 4 hours ⚹ Ideal slow-cooker size: 6-qt.

I cup sliced fresh mushrooms
I large sweet onion, chopped
½ cup chopped red bell pepper
3 cloves garlic, chopped
I Tbsp. butter
I Tbsp. olive oil
I large head broccoli, chopped
½ cup diced Parmesan cheese
I tsp. dried basil
½ tsp. dried oregano
Salt and pepper, to taste
Juice and zest of I lemon

1. Sprinkle mushrooms, onion, bell pepper, and garlic into crock, sprinkled lightly with salt and pepper. Dot with butter and drizzle with olive oil.

2. Sprinkle in broccoli and diced Parmesan. Sprinkle with basil and oregano, adding salt and pepper to taste.

3. Cover and cook on Low for 4 hours.

4. Drizzle with lemon juice and zest before serving.

Serving suggestion:
Serve over cauliflower rice.

- Calories 91
- Fat 6
- Sodium 134
- Carbs 6
- Sugar 1.5
- Protein 3.5

Golden Cauliflower

Carol Peachey, Lancaster, PA

Makes 6 servings
Prep. Time: 15 minutes   ❧   Cooking Time: 3½–5 hours   ❧   Ideal slow-cooker size: 4-qt.

2 (10-oz.) pkgs. frozen cauliflower, thawed

2 Tbsp. butter, melted

1 Tbsp. almond flour

1 cup evaporated milk

1 oz. (¼ cup) cheddar cheese

2 Tbsp. cottage cheese

2 tsp. Parmesan cheese

4 slices bacon, crisply browned and crumbled

1. Place cauliflower in slow cooker.

2. Melt butter on stove. Add almond flour and evaporated milk. Heat till thickened. Add cheeses.

3. Pour sauce over cauliflower. Top with bacon.

4. Cover. Cook on High 1½ hours and then reduce to Low for an additional 2 hours. Or cook only on Low 4–5 hours.

- Calories 175
- Fat 12
- Sodium 253
- Carbs 10
- Sugar 6
- Protein 9

Country Market Cauliflower

Susie Shenk Wenger, Lancaster, PA

Makes 6 servings
Prep. Time: 20 minutes ⚓ Cooking Time: 2–4 hours ⚓ Ideal slow-cooker size: 5- or 6-qt.

1 Tbsp. butter

1 Tbsp. olive oil

Juice of 1 lemon

8 oz. fresh baby bella mushrooms, sliced

1 large Vidalia or candy sweet onion, chopped

½ cup red or yellow bell pepper

1 large head cauliflower, cut in pieces

3 cloves garlic, crushed

1 tsp. dried basil

Salt and pepper, to taste

½ cup grated Parmesan cheese

1. Sauté mushrooms, onion, and bell pepper in a pan with olive oil and butter with the lemon juice.

2. Place cauliflower, garlic, basil, salt and pepper in a greased 5- or 6-quart slow cooker.

3. Stir in sautéed vegetable mixture.

4. Cook on Low, covered, for 2–4 hours, or until cauliflower is as tender as you like it.

5. Top with Parmesan cheese just before serving, while still hot.

- Calories 131
- Fat 6
- Sodium 139
- Carbs 6
- Sugar 2
- Protein 4

Cabbage Casserole

Edwina Stoltzfus, Narvon, PA

Makes 6 servings
Prep. Time: 40 minutes ⚜ *Cooking Time: 4–5 hours* ⚜ *Ideal slow-cooker size: 4-qt.*

1 large head cabbage, chopped
2 cups water
3 Tbsp. butter
¼ cup almond flour
¼ tsp. salt
¼ tsp. pepper
1⅓ cups milk
1⅓ cups shredded cheddar cheese

1. Cook cabbage in saucepan in boiling water for 5 minutes. Drain. Place in slow cooker.

2. In saucepan, melt butter. Stir in flour, salt, and pepper. Add milk, stirring constantly on Low heat for 5 minutes. Remove from heat. Stir in cheese. Pour over cabbage.

3. Cover. Cook on Low 4–5 hours.

- Calories 204
- Fat 18
- Sodium 266
- Carbs 4
- Sugar 2.5
- Protein 8

Scalloped Cabbage

Edwina Stoltzfus, Lebanon, PA

Makes 6–8 servings
Prep. Time: 25 minutes   ⚘   Cooking Time: 3–5 hours   ⚘   Ideal slow-cooker size: 4-qt.

1 Tbsp. butter

12 cups chopped cabbage

¼ cup chopped onion

¼ cup chopped fresh parsley

1 cup grated sharp cheese

¼ cup almond flour

12-oz. can evaporated milk

½ cup diced, cooked bacon, *optional*

1. Use butter to grease slow cooker.

2. Combine cabbage, onion, parsley, and cheese in slow cooker.

3. In a mixing bowl, whisk together almond flour and milk until lump free.

4. Pour milk mixture over cabbage mixture.

5. Cover and cook on Low for 3–5 hours, until cabbage is soft and sauce is thick.

6. Sprinkle with bacon if you wish before serving.

NOTE
If you're adding bacon to the top, use bacon grease instead of butter to grease the crock. Add 1 tsp. of your favorite dried herb.

- Calories 177
- Fat 11
- Sodium 160
- Carbs 12
- Sugar 8
- Protein 9

Fast and Fabulous Brussels Sprouts

Phyllis Good, Lancaster, PA

Makes 4–6 servings
Prep. Time: 15 minutes & Cooking Time: 2–5 hours & Ideal slow-cooker size: 2- or 3-qt.

1 lb. Brussels sprouts, bottoms trimmed off and halved

3 Tbsp. butter, melted

1½ Tbsp. Dijon mustard

¼ tsp. salt

¼ tsp. freshly ground black pepper

¼ cup water

½ tsp. dried tarragon, *optional*

1. Mix all ingredients in slow cooker.

2. Cover and cook on High for 2–2½ hours, or Low for 4–5 hours, until sprouts are just soft. Some of the Brussels sprouts at the sides will get brown and crispy, and this is delicious.

3. Stir well to distribute sauce. Serve hot or warm.

- Calories 84
- Fat 6
- Sodium 186
- Carbs 7
- Sugar 2
- Protein 3

Brussel Sprouts with Pimentos

Donna Lantgon, Rapid City, SD

Makes 8 servings

Prep. Time: 10 minutes   *Cooking Time: 6 hours*   *Ideal slow-cooker size: 3½- or 4-qt.*

2 lb. Brussels sprouts

¼ tsp. dried oregano

½ tsp. dried basil

2-oz. jar pimentos, drained

¼ cup, or I small can, sliced black olives, drained

I Tbsp. olive oil

½ cup water

1. Combine all ingredients in slow cooker.

2. Cook on Low 6 hours, or until sprouts are just tender.

- Calories 71
- Fat 2.5
- Sodium 61
- Carbs 11
- Sugar 3
- Protein 4

Very Special Spinach

Jeanette Oberholtzer, Manheim, PA

Makes 8 servings
Prep. Time: 10 minutes ❧ Cooking Time: 5 hours ❧ Ideal slow-cooker size: 4-qt.

3 10-oz. boxes frozen spinach, thawed and drained

2 cups cottage cheese

1½ cups grated cheddar cheese

3 eggs

¼ cup almond flour

1 tsp. salt

8 Tbsp. butter, melted

1. Mix together all ingredients.

2. Pour into slow cooker.

3. Cook on High 1 hour. Reduce heat to Low and cook 4 more hours.

- Calories 316
- Fat 25
- Sodium 677
- Carbs 8
- Sugar 2
- Protein 18

Creamed Spinach

Mary Reichert, O'Fallon, MO

Makes 4 servings
Prep. Time: 10 minutes   ❧   Cooking Time: 2–3 hours   ❧   Ideal slow-cooker size: 3-qt.

2 (10-oz.) boxes frozen spinach, thawed and drained

¼ cup dried onion flakes

2 Tbsp. low-sodium beef bouillon granules

¼ tsp. onion powder

¼ tsp. parsley flakes

⅛ tsp. celery seed

⅛ tsp. paprika

⅛ tsp. black pepper

1 cup sour cream

8-oz. can water chestnuts, chopped, *optional*

1. In a mixing bowl, mix spinach, dehydrated onions, beef bouillon granules, onion powder, parsley flakes, celery seed, paprika, black pepper, and sour cream. Add water chestnuts if using. Blend well.

2. Spray 3-quart slow cooker with cooking spray. Add spinach mixture and top with cheese.

3. Cook on Low 2–3 hours, until bubbly.

- Calories 158
- Fat 10
- Sodium 258
- Carbs 13
- Sugar 4
- Protein 7

Caponata

Katrine Rose, Woodbridge, VA

Makes 10 servings
Prep. Time: 20 minutes ⚶ *Cooking Time: 7–8 hours* ⚶ *Ideal slow-cooker size: 4-qt.*

1 medium (1-lb.) eggplant, peeled and cut into ½-inch cubes

14-oz. can diced tomatoes

1 medium onion, chopped

1 red bell pepper, cut into ½-inch pieces

¾ cup salsa

¼ cup olive oil

2 Tbsp. capers, drained

3 Tbsp. balsamic vinegar

3 cloves garlic, minced

1¼ tsp. dried oregano

⅓ cup, packed, chopped fresh basil

1. Combine all ingredients except basil in slow cooker.

2. Cover. Cook on Low 7–8 hours, or until vegetables are tender.

3. Stir in basil.

- Calories 85
- Fat 6
- Sodium 244
- Carbs 8
- Sugar 3
- Protein 1

Zucchini in Sour Cream

Lizzie Ann Yoder, Hartville, OH

Makes 6 servings
Prep. Time: 20 minutes   ♣   Cooking Time: 1–1½ hours   ♣   Ideal slow-cooker size: 3- or 4-qt.

4 cups unpeeled, sliced zucchini

I cup sour cream

¼ cup whole milk

I cup chopped onions

I tsp. salt

I cup grated sharp cheddar cheese

1. Cook zucchini in microwave on High 2–3 minutes. Turn into slow cooker sprayed with cooking spray.

2. Combine sour cream, milk, onions, and salt. Pour over zucchini and stir gently.

3. Cover. Cook on Low 1–1½ hours.

4. Sprinkle cheese over vegetables 30 minutes before serving.

- Calories 169
- Fat 13
- Sodium 464
- Carbs 7
- Sugar 5
- Protein 7

Fresh Zucchini and Tomatoes

Pauline Morrison, St. Marys, ON

Makes 6–8 servings

Prep. Time: 15 minutes   &   Cooking Time: 2½–3 hours   &   Ideal slow-cooker size: 3½-qt.

1½ lb. zucchini, peeled if you wish, and cut into ¼-inch slices

19-oz. can stewed tomatoes, broken up and undrained

1½ cloves garlic, minced

½ tsp. salt

1½ Tbsp. butter

1. Place zucchini slices in slow cooker.

2. Add tomatoes, garlic, and salt. Mix well.

3. Dot surface with butter.

4. Cover and cook on High 2½–3 hours, or until zucchini are done to your liking.

- Calories 88
- Fat 4
- Sodium 433
- Carbs 12
- Sugar 4
- Protein 2

Pizza-Style Zucchini

Marcella Roberts, Denver, PA

Makes 6 servings
Prep. Time: 20 minutes ☙ Cooking Time: 2½ hours ☙ Ideal slow-cooker size: 4-qt.

2 medium zucchini, unpeeled and cut in disks

2 medium yellow squash, unpeeled and cut in disks

½ cup tomato sauce

¾ tsp. Italian seasoning

5 drops liquid stevia

½ tsp. garlic powder

½ tsp. onion powder

1 large tomato, diced

1 cup grated mozzarella cheese

Sliced black olives, *optional*

1. Layer zucchini and squash in lightly greased slow cooker, alternating colors.

2. Mix together the tomato sauce, Italian seasoning, liquid stevia, garlic powder, and onion powder. Stir in the tomato. Pour over zucchini and yellow squash.

3. Sprinkle with mozzarella and black olives (if using).

4. Cover and cook on High for 2 hours, until bubbly. Remove lid and cook an additional 30 minutes on High to evaporate some of the liquid.

TIP
Add basil, oregano, and chopped garlic if you want to really amp up the pizza flavor.

- Calories 63
- Fat 3
- Sodium 215
- Carbs 4
- Sugar 2
- Protein 5

Southern Green Beans

Pat Bishop, Bedminster, PA

Makes 4–6 servings
Prep. Time: 10 minutes ⚜ *Cooking Time: 2–4 hours* ⚜ *Ideal slow-cooker size: 3- to 4-qt.*

2 cups chicken bone broth

1 lb. fresh or frozen cut green beans

1 cup chopped onion

½ cup cooked, chopped bacon

1 Tbsp. white vinegar

1 Tbsp. liquid aminos

¼ tsp. pepper

1 clove garlic, minced

1. Toss all ingredients together in slow cooker.

2. Cover and cook on Low for 4 hours or on High for 2 hours.

- Calories 170
- Fat 9
- Sodium 663
- Carbs 12
- Sugar 5
- Protein 11

Dutch Green Beans

Edwina Stoltzfus, Narvon, PA

Makes 4–6 servings
Prep. Time: 20 minutes ⚶ Cooking Time: 4½ hours ⚶ Ideal slow-cooker size: 4- to 5-qt.

½ lb. bacon, or ham chunks

4 medium onions, sliced

2 qts. fresh, or frozen green beans

4 cups canned stewed tomatoes, or diced fresh tomatoes

½–¾ tsp. salt

¼ tsp. pepper

1. Brown bacon until crisp in skillet. Drain, reserving 2 Tbsp. drippings. Crumble bacon into small pieces.

2. Sauté onions in bacon drippings.

3. Combine all ingredients in slow cooker.

4. Cover. Cook on Low 4½ hours.

- Calories 151
- Fat 3
- Sodium 760
- Carbs 22
- Sugar 8
- Protein 12

Green Beans with Tomato, Bacon, and Onions

Hope Comerford, Clinton Township, MI

Makes 4 servings
Prep. Time: 10 minutes ☙ Cooking Time: 4 hours ☙ Ideal slow-cooker size: 2-qt.

2½–3 cups fresh green beans, ends snapped off, washed and halved

2 small tomatoes, chopped

1 small onion, chopped

3 Tbsp. fresh bacon pieces

1 tsp. onion powder

1 tsp. garlic powder

½ tsp. salt

⅛ tsp. red pepper

½ cup chicken bone broth

1. Add all ingredients to the crock and give it a stir.

2. Cover and cook on Low for 4 hours.

- Calories 49
- Fat 1
- Sodium 349
- Carbs 8
- Sugar 4
- Protein 4

Baked Tomatoes

Lizzie Ann Yoder, Hartville, OH

Makes 4 servings
Prep. Time: 10 minutes ⚬ *Cooking Time: 45 minutes–1 hour* ⚬ *Ideal slow-cooker size: 2½- or 3-qt.*

2 tomatoes, each cut in half

½ Tbsp. olive oil

½ tsp. parsley, chopped, or ¼ tsp. dry parsley flakes

¼ tsp. dried oregano

¼ tsp. dried basil

1. Spray slow cooker crock with cooking spray Place tomato halves in crock.

2. Drizzle oil over tomatoes. Sprinkle with remaining ingredients.

3. Cover. Cook on High 45 minutes–1 hour.

- Calories 26
- Fat 2
- Sodium 3
- Carbs 2
- Sugar 2
- Protein 1

Wild Mushrooms Italian

Connie Johnson, Loudon, NH

Makes 4–5 servings

Prep. Time: 20 minutes ♣ *Cooking Time: 6–8 hours* ♣ *Ideal slow-cooker size: 5-qt.*

2 large onions, chopped

3 large red bell peppers, chopped

3 large green bell peppers, chopped

2–3 Tbsp. olive oil

12-oz. pkg. oyster mushrooms, cleaned and chopped

4 cloves garlic, minced

3 fresh bay leaves

10 fresh basil leaves, chopped

1 Tbsp. salt

1 ½ tsp. pepper

28-oz. can Italian plum tomatoes, crushed, or chopped

1. Sauté onions and peppers in oil in skillet until soft. Stir in mushrooms and garlic. Sauté just until mushrooms begin to turn brown. Pour into slow cooker.

2. Add remaining ingredients. Stir well.

3. Cover. Cook on Low 6–8 hours.

- Calories 171
- Fat 9
- Sodium 410
- Carbs 22
- Sugar 10
- Protein 5

Lemony Garlic Asparagus

Hope Comerford, Clinton Township, MI

Makes 4 servings
Prep. Time: 5 minutes & Cooking Time: 1½–2 hours & Ideal slow-cooker size: 2- or 3-qt.

1 lb. asparagus, bottom inch (tough part) removed

1 Tbsp. olive oil

1½ Tbsp. lemon juice

3–4 cloves garlic, peeled and minced

¼ tsp. salt

⅛ tsp. pepper

1. Spray crock with nonstick spray.

2. Lay asparagus at bottom of crock and coat with the olive oil.

3. Pour the lemon juice over the top, then sprinkle with the garlic, salt, and pepper.

4. Cover and cook on Low for 1½–2 hours.

Serving suggestion:

Garnish with diced pimento, garlic, and lemon zest.

- Calories 58
- Fat 3.5
- Sodium 123
- Carbs 6
- Sugar 2
- Protein 3

Slow Cooker Beets

Hope Comerford, Clinton Township, MI

Makes 4–6 servings
Prep. Time: 10 minutes & Cooking Time: 3–4 hours & Ideal slow-cooker size: 3-qt.

4–6 large beets, scrubbed well and tops removed

3 Tbsp. olive oil

I tsp. sea salt

¼ tsp. pepper

3 Tbsp. balsamic vinegar

I Tbsp. lemon juice

1. Use foil to make a packet around each beet.

2. Divide the olive oil, salt, pepper, balsamic vinegar, and lemon juice evenly between each packet.

3. Place each beet packet into the slow cooker.

4. Cover and cook on Low for 3–4 hours, or until the beets are tender when poked with a knife.

5. Remove each beet packet from the crock and allow to cool and let the steam escape. Once cool enough to handle, use a paring knife to gently peel the skin off each beet. Cut into bite-sized pieces and serve with juice from the packet over the top.

- Calories 103
- Fat 7
- Sodium 426
- Carbs 10
- Sugar 7
- Protein 1

Raspberry Almond Bars

Makes 24 servings

Prep. Time: 20–30 minutes ⚬ *Cooking Time: 2½–3 hours* ⚬ *Ideal slow-cooker size: oval 6-qt.*

1 ½ cups almond flour

¼ cup flaxseed

12 packets stevia

8 Tbsp. (1 stick) butter, softened

½ tsp. almond extract

½ cup low-carb, no-sugar raspberry preserves

⅓ cup sliced almonds

TIP

Watch for the raspberry preserves to ooze out around the edges as these bars bake!

- Calories 97
- Fat 9
- Sodium 3
- Carbs 4
- Sugar 0
- Protein 2

1. Grease interior of slow cooker crock.

2. In a large bowl, combine flour, flaxseed, and stevia.

3. Cut in butter with a pastry cutter or two knives—or your fingers—until mixture forms coarse crumbs.

4. Stir in extract until well blended.

5. Set aside 1 cup crumbs.

6. Press remaining crumbs into bottom of crock.

7. Spread preserves over crust to within ½ inch of the edges (the preserves could burn if they touch the hot crock).

8. In a small bowl, combine reserved 1 cup crumbs with almonds. Sprinkle evenly over preserves, pressing down gently to hold the almonds in place.

9. Cover. Bake on High for 2½–3 hours, or until firm in center.

10. Uncover. Lift crock onto wire baking rack to cool.

11. When room temperature, cut bars into 20 squares, and 4 triangles in the corners.

Lotsa Chocolate Almond Cake

Hope Comerford, Clinton Township, MI

Makes 10 servings

Prep. Time: 10 minutes & Cooking Time: 3 hours & Cooling Time: 30 minutes & Ideal slow-cooker size: 6-qt.

1½ cups almond flour

18 packets stevia

⅔ cup unsweetened cocoa powder

¼ cup keto-friendly chocolate protein powder

2 tsp. baking powder

¼ tsp. salt

½ cup coconut oil, melted

4 eggs

¾ cup almond milk

1 tsp. vanilla extract

1 tsp. almond extract

¾ cup chopped 90% dark chocolate

1. Cover any hot spot of your crock with aluminum foil and spray crock with nonstick spray.

2. In a bowl, mix together the almond flour, stevia, cocoa powder, protein powder, baking powder, and salt.

3. In a different bowl, mix together the coconut oil, eggs, almond milk, and vanilla and almond extracts.

4. Pour wet ingredients into dry ingredients and mix until well-combined. Stir in chopped chocolate.

5. Pour cake mix into crock. Cover and cook on Low for 3 hours.

6. Turn the slow cooker off when the cooking time is over and let the cake cool in the crock for 30 minutes.

7. Place a plate or platter over the crock, then turn the crock upside down on the plate, so the cake releases onto the plate or platter.

- Calories 108
- Fat 31
- Sodium 191
- Carbs 26
- Sugar 9
- Protein 11

Fudgy Secret Brownies

Juanita Weaver, Johnsonville, IL

Makes 8 servings
Prep. Time: 10 minutes ⚘ *Cooking Time: 1½–2 hours* ⚘ *Ideal slow cooker size: 6- or 7-qt.*

4 oz. unsweetened chocolate

¾ cup coconut oil

¾ cup frozen diced okra, partially thawed

3 large eggs

36 stevia packets

1 teaspoon pure vanilla extract

¼ tsp. mineral salt

¾ cup coconut flour

½–¾ cup coarsely chopped walnuts or pecans, *optional*

1. Melt chocolate and coconut oil in small saucepan.

2. Put okra and eggs in blender. Blend until smooth.

3. Measure all other ingredients in mixing bowl.

4. Pour melted chocolate and okra over the dry ingredients and stir with fork just until mixed.

5. Pour into greased slow cooker.

6. Cover and cook on High for 1½–2 hours.

- Calories 421
- Fat 38
- Sodium 113
- Carbs 15
- Sugar 1
- Protein 8

Black and Blue Cobbler

Renee Shirk, Mount Joy, PA

Makes 6 servings
Prep. Time: 20 minutes ☙ Cooking Time: 2–2½ hours ☙ Ideal slow-cooker size: 5-qt.

1 cup almond flour
36 packets stevia, *divided*
1 tsp. baking powder
¼ tsp. salt
¼ tsp. ground cinnamon
¼ tsp. ground nutmeg
2 eggs, beaten
2 Tbsp. whole milk
2 Tbsp. coconut oil, melted
2 cups fresh, or frozen, blueberries
2 cups fresh, or frozen, blackberries
¾ cup water
1 tsp. grated orange peel

1. Combine almond flour, 18 packets stevia, baking powder, salt, cinnamon, and nutmeg.

2. Combine eggs, milk, and oil. Stir into dry ingredients until moistened.

3. Spread the batter evenly over bottom of greased slow cooker.

4. In saucepan, combine berries, water, orange peel, and remaining 18 packets stevia. Bring to boil. Remove from heat and pour over batter. Cover.

5. Cook on High 2–2½ hours, or until toothpick inserted into batter comes out clean. Turn off cooker.

6. Uncover and let stand 30 minutes before serving.

- Calories 224
- Fat 16
- Sodium 174
- Carbs 21
- Sugar 8
- Protein 7

Slow Cooker Crème Brûlée

Makes 4–6 servings

Prep. Time: 20 minutes & *Cooking Time: 2–4 hours* & *Chilling Time: 4 hours*
Ideal slow-cooker size: oval 6-qt.

5 egg yolks

2 cups heavy cream

¼ cup erythritol

1 Tbsp. high-quality vanilla extract

Pinch salt

2 Tbsp. powdered erythitol

Fresh berries, to garnish

TIP

This is a perfect summer dessert if you don't have an ice-cream maker but still want to make something cold and creamy.

- Calories 323
- Fat 33
- Sodium 28
- Carbs 11
- Sugar 3
- Protein 4.5

1. Get a baking dish that fits in your slow cooker. Put it in the slow cooker and pour water around it until the water comes halfway up the sides of the dish. Push the dish down if you need to (as it would be when it's full of the Crème Brûlée), to see the water level. Remove the dish and set aside.

2. In medium mixing bowl, beat egg yolks.

3. Slowly pour in cream and erythitol while mixing. Add vanilla and salt.

4. Pour mixture into the baking dish.

5. Carefully place dish into water in slow cooker, being careful not to get water in the cream mixture.

6. Cover cooker and cook on High for 2–4 hours, until set but still a little jiggly in the middle.

7. Very carefully remove hot dish from hot slow cooker and let it cool on the counter. Refrigerate for 2 hours.

8. Sprinkle the powdered erythitol evenly over the top. Broil for 3–10 minutes, until the sugar is bubbly and browning. Watch carefully! Or if you own a kitchen torch, use that instead to caramelize the sugar.

9. Return Crème Brûlée to refrigerator for at least 2 more hours. Serve cold with a few beautiful berries to garnish.

Baked Custard

Barbara Smith, Bedford, PA

Makes 5–6 servings

Prep Time: 10–15 minutes ❧ *Cooking Time: 2–3 hours* ❧ *Ideal slow-cooker size: 4- to 5-qt.*

2 cups whole milk

3 eggs, slightly beaten

2½ Tsp., plus ¼ tsp., erythritol, *divided*

I tsp. vanilla extract

¼ tsp. cinnamon

1. Heat milk in a small uncovered saucepan until a skin forms on top. Remove from heat and let cool slightly.

2. Meanwhile, in a large mixing bowl combine eggs, 2½ Tbsp. erythritol, and vanilla.

3. Slowly stir cooled milk into egg-erythritol mixture.

4. Pour into a greased 1-qt. baking dish which will fit into your slow cooker, or into a baking insert designed for your slow cooker.

5. Mix cinnamon and ½ tsp. reserved erythritol in a small bowl. Sprinkle over custard mixture.

6. Cover baking dish or insert with foil. Set container on a metal rack or trivet in slow cooker. Pour hot water around dish to a depth of 1 inch.

7. Cover cooker. Cook on High 2–3 hours, or until custard is set. (When blade of a knife inserted in center of custard comes out clean, custard is set.)

8. Serve warm from baking dish or insert.

- Calories 254
- Fat 3
- Sodium 6
- Carbs 52
- Sugar 11
- Protein 4

Variations:

Instead of the cinnamon, use ¼ tsp. nutmeg, or 1–2 Tbsp. grated coconut.

Simple Egg Custard

Paula Winchester, Kansas City, MO

Makes 6 servings

Prep. Time: 25 minutes & Cooking Time: 2–3 hours & Ideal slow-cooker size: 6-qt.

1 ½ cups whole milk

1 cup half-and-half

3 eggs

3 Tbsp. erythritol

½ tsp. vanilla extract

Pinch salt

Variations:

May use 4–5 baking ramekins instead of 1 shallow baking dish.

Serving suggestion:

Serve with fresh berries on top.

1. In mixing bowl, whisk ingredients well until smooth and totally combined.

2. Prepare slow cooker by finding a shallow oval baking dish that can fit inside. Place jar rings or lids or trivets on the floor of the crock so the baking dish is not touching the bottom or sides of the crock.

3. Pour custard liquid in baking dish. Set in crock.

4. Carefully pour water into the crock (not the baking dish!) to reach halfway up the side of the baking dish.

5. Cover slow cooker. Cook on High for 2–4 hours, or until custard is set in the middle.

6. Wearing oven gloves to protect your knuckles, remove baking dish from cooker. Allow to cool for at least 20 minutes before serving warm. May also serve chilled.

TIPS

There are different ways to flavor the custard. Heat the milk and add 1 bay leaf. Allow to steep and cool. Remove bay leaf and proceed with Step 1. Alternatively, sprinkle top of Custard with ½ tsp. ground nutmeg or cinnamon in Step 3.

- Calories 132
- Fat 9
- Sodium 86
- Carbs 11
- Sugar 4
- Protein 6

Berries Jubilee

Hope Comerford, Clinton Township, MI

Makes 4 servings
Prep. Time: 15 minutes & Cooking Time: 3–4 hours & Ideal slow-cooker size: 2-to- 3-qt.

I lb. fresh cherries, pitted

¼ cup erythritol

I tsp. lemon juice

I tsp. lemon zest

I tsp. vanilla extract

⅓ cup rum

2 Tbsp. flaxseed

2 Tbsp. water

1. Spray crock with nonstick spray.

2. Place cherries in crock with erythritol, lemon juice, lemon zest, vanilla, and rum.

3. Mix together the flaxseed and water, then stir this into the contents of the crock.

4. Cook on Low for 3–4 hours.

- Calories 254
- Fat 3
- Sodium 6
- Carbs 52
- Sugar 11
- Protein 4

Raspberry Custard

Makes 6 servings

Prep. Time: 15 minutes ❧ *Cooking Time: 3–4 hours* ❧ *Standing Time: 30–60 minutes*
Ideal slow-cooker size: 4-qt.

5 eggs

¼ cup erythritol

½ tsp. salt

¾ cup almond flour

12-oz. can evaporated milk

1 tsp. vanilla extract

Pinch cinnamon

2 Tbsp. butter

2 cups red raspberries, fresh or frozen, thawed and drained

1. Beat eggs, erythritol, and salt in mixing bowl until eggs no longer cling to whisk.

2. Add flour in three portions, whisking well after each addition until no lumps remain.

3. Whisk in evaporated milk, vanilla, and cinnamon.

4. Use butter to generously grease slow cooker.

5. Pour egg mixture into cooker. Sprinkle evenly with raspberries.

6. Cover and cook on Low for 3–4 hours, until set.

7. Remove lid and allow to cool for 30–60 minutes before serving. May chill before serving as well.

- Calories 273
- Fat 19
- Sodium 285
- Carbs 22
- Sugar 8
- Protein 13

Maple Pot de Crème

Phyllis Good, Lancaster, PA

Makes 4–6 servings
Prep. Time: 10 minutes ⚜ Cooking Time: 2–3 hours ⚜ Chilling Time: at least 2 hours
Standing Time: about 1 hour ⚜ Ideal slow-cooker size: 6-qt.

2 egg yolks

2 eggs

1 cup heavy cream

½ cup whole milk

½ cup plus 1 Tbsp. Sukrin Gold

Pinch salt

1 tsp. vanilla extract

¼ tsp. ground nutmeg

Whipped cream, for garnish, *optional*

1. In a mixing bowl, beat egg yolks and eggs until light and frothy.

2. Add cream, milk, 1 Tbsp. Sukrin Gold, salt, vanilla, and nutmeg. Mix well.

3. Get a baking dish that fits in your slow cooker.

4. Pour mixture in baking dish and set it in slow cooker.

5. Carefully pour water around the baking dish until the water comes halfway up the sides.

6. Cover cooker. Cook on High for 2–3 hours, until Pot de Crème is set but still a little bit jiggly in the middle.

7. Wearing oven mitts to protect your knuckles, carefully remove hot dish from cooker. Set on wire rack to cool to room temperature.

8. Cover tightly and chill for at least 2 hours before serving. Garnish with whipped cream if you wish.

NOTE

Want an impressive, special dessert with very little effort? This is it! The texture is luscious, the flavor is delightful, and you can dress it up with fresh berries.

- Calories 102
- Fat 18
- Sodium 46
- Carbs 12
- Sugar 2
- Protein 5

Slow-Cooker Pumpkin Pie Pudding

Joette Droz, Kalona, IA

Makes 4–6 servings
Prep. Time: 5–7 minutes ⚶ *Cooking Time: 6–7 hours* ⚶ *Ideal slow-cooker size: 3-qt.*

15-oz. can solid pack pumpkin
12-oz. can evaporated milk
¼ cup plus 2 Tbsp. erythritol
½ cup keto-friendly baking mix
2 eggs, beaten
2 Tbsp. melted butter
1 Tbsp. pumpkin pie spice
2 tsp. vanilla extract

1. Mix together all ingredients. Pour into greased slow cooker.

2. Cover and cook on Low 6–7 hours, or until thermometer reads 160°F.

- Calories 168
- Fat 15
- Sodium 91
- Carbs 22
- Sugar 3
- Protein 9

Metric Equivalent Measurements

If you're accustomed to using metric measurements, I don't want you to be inconvenienced by the imperial measurements I use in this book.

Use this handy chart, too, to figure out the size of the slow cooker you'll need for each recipe.

Weight (Dry Ingredients)

1 oz		30 g
4 oz	¼ lb	120 g
8 oz	½ lb	240 g
12 oz	¾ lb	360 g
16 oz	1 lb	480 g
32 oz	2 lb	960 g

Slow Cooker Sizes

1-quart	0.96 l
2-quart	1.92 l
3-quart	2.88 l
4-quart	3.84 l
5-quart	4.80 l
6-quart	5.76 l
7-quart	6.72 l
8-quart	7.68 l

Volume (Liquid Ingredients)

½ tsp.		2 ml
1 tsp.		5 ml
1 Tbsp.	½ fl oz	15 ml
2 Tbsp.	1 fl oz	30 ml
¼ cup	2 fl oz	60 ml
⅓ cup	3 fl oz	80 ml
½ cup	4 fl oz	120 ml
⅔ cup	5 fl oz	160 ml
¾ cup	6 fl oz	180 ml
1 cup	8 fl oz	240 ml
1 pt	16 fl oz	480 ml
1 qt	32 fl oz	960 ml

Length

¼ in	6 mm
½ in	13 mm
¾ in	19 mm
1 in	25 mm
6 in	15 cm
12 in	30 cm

Recipe and Ingredient Index

About the Author

Hope Comerford is a mom, wife, elementary music teacher, blogger, recipe developer, public speaker, ALM Zone fit leader, Young Living Essential Oils essential oil enthusiast/educator, and published author. In 2013, she was diagnosed with a severe gluten intolerance and since then has spent many hours creating easy, practical, and delicious gluten-free recipes that can be enjoyed by both those who are affected by gluten and those who are not.

Growing up, Hope spent many hours in the kitchen with her Meme (grandmother) and her love for cooking grew from there. While working on her master's degree when her daughter was young, Hope turned to her slow cookers for some salvation and sanity. It was from there she began truly experimenting with recipes and quickly learned she had the ability to get a little more creative in the kitchen and develop her own recipes.

In 2010, Hope started her blog, *A Busy Mom's Slow Cooker Adventures*, to simply share the recipes she was making with her family and friends. She never imagined people all over the world would begin visiting her page and sharing her recipes with others as well. In 2013, Hope self-published her first cookbook, *Slow Cooker Recipes 10 Ingredients or Less and Gluten-Free*, and then later wrote *The Gluten-Free Slow Cooker*.

Hope became the new brand ambassador and author of Fix-It and Forget-It in mid-2016. Since then, she has brought her excitement and creativeness to the Fix-It and Forget-It brand. Through Fix-It and Forget-It, she has written *Fix-It and Forget-It Lazy & Slow, Fix-It and Forget-It Healthy Slow Cooker Cookbook, Forget-It Cooking for Two, Fix-It and Forget-It Instant Pot Cookbook*, and *Fix-It and Forget-It Freezer Meals*.

Hope lives in the city of Clinton Township, Michigan, near Metro Detroit. Hope is a native of Michigan and has lived there her whole life. She has been happily married to her husband and best friend, Justin, since 2008. Together they have two children, Ella and Gavin, who are her motivation, inspiration, and heart. In her spare time, Hope enjoys traveling, singing, cooking, reading books, spending time with friends and family, and relaxing.